Edward de Bono studied at Christ Church, Oxford (as a Rhodes Scholar). He also holds a PhD from Cambridge and an MD from the University of Malta. He has held appointments at the universities of Oxford, London, Cambridge and Harvard.

In 1967 de Bono invented the now commonly used term 'lateral thinking' and, for many thousands, indeed millions, of people worldwide, his name has since become a symbol of creativity and new thinking. He has written numerous books, which have been translated into 34 languages, and his advice is sought by Nobel laureates and world leaders alike.

THE MECHANISM OF MIND

UNDERSTAND HOW YOUR MIND WORKS TO MAXIMISE MEMORY AND CREATIVE POTENTIAL

EDWARD DE BONO

Vermilion
LONDON

1 3 5 7 9 10 8 6 4 2

Vermilion, an imprint of Ebury Publishing,
20 Vauxhall Bridge Road,
London SW1V 2SA

Vermilion is part of the Penguin Random House group of companies
whose addresses can be found at global.penguinrandomhouse.com

Penguin
Random House
UK

For enquiries please contact de Bono Global Pty Ltd
www.debono.com

First published by Vermilion in 2015
First published by Jonathan Cape Ltd in 1969

www.eburypublishing.co.uk

A CIP catalogue record for this book is available
from the British Library

ISBN 9781785040085

Printed and bound in Great Britain by Clays Ltd, St Ives PLC

Penguin Random House is committed to a sustainable future for our
business, our readers and our planet. This book is made from Forest
Stewardship Council® certified paper.

MIX
Paper from
responsible sources
FSC® C018179

CONTENTS

PART 2

INTRODUCTION

There are those who suppose that the brain will for ever remain a mystery. There are those who suppose that one day the way the brain works will be revealed in all its detail. Of what use would such knowledge be? Would the problems of mankind be suddenly solved by a surge of understanding? Would one be able to make practical use of the knowledge?

This book is to do with the way the brain becomes mind. It may be that the brain is not too difficult to understand, but too easy. Matters are often made more and more complex by the ability of man to play elaborate games that feed on themselves to create bewildering structures of immense intricacy, which obscure rather than reveal. The only thing these structures do reveal is that man has the ability and the compulsion to play such conceptual games. Indeed, it is the nature of the brain with which he is examining the brain that makes him do so. Ideas must advance; if they miss the right direction they move farther and farther in the wrong direction. In matters of introspection, movement is unlimited. The track can never run out, since it is created by the moving imagination, just as there are military vehicles which lay down their own track ahead of them as they cross trackless swamps.

Of its own accord the brain does not seek to understand and explain, but to create explanations – and that is a very different thing. The explanations may be highly acceptable without having much relevance to what is being explained. Can one escape from the circular self-satisfaction of elaborate philosophical description? In this book the brain is described as the mechanical behaviour of mechanical units. It is the organization of these units that provides the mechanism of mind.

Why does one bother to think about things, to talk about things, to write about things? Why does one imagine that other people ought to be interested in what is being said or what has been written? If one is describing something, then one hopes that the beauty of the description may be appreciated. Even in a description one may seek to reveal something that one supposes not to be apparent to everyone else. As one seeks to reveal more, so one moves from description towards explanation. In explanation one tries to reveal how something unfamiliar is only a special arrangement of things that are already familiar. We do know how these familiar things work, so we can tell how the unfamiliar whole must work. We want to know how it works in order to make better use of it, perhaps change it, perhaps improve it, perhaps prevent it going wrong, perhaps repair it. Above all, we usually want to be able to tell how it is going to behave in general and also under special circumstances. If the purpose of description is beauty, the purpose of explanation is usefulness. To say that a lawn undulates is description; to discover the buried tree roots is an explanation which may bring about their removal.

It is for the reader and not the writer to assess the usefulness of what is set down in this book. Nevertheless, it is possible to point to one definite and very practical example of the usefulness of the explanation offered.

Words usually describe things or actions, which are just things in motion. There are, however, a few words which do not describe things, but which provide tools for dealing with other words. Multiplication, division, addition and subtraction are special ways of dealing with quantities. Each of these processes is represented by a symbol which becomes a tool for carrying out the process. Words like 'not' and 'if' are tools for dealing with other words and carrying out certain processes. In this book a new tool is suggested. This is a new word which does not yet exist in any language. It is used to carry out a process which cannot otherwise be performed. Once this word has been invented and its function defined, then people can become as accustomed to using it as they are accustomed to using the word 'not'. When this happens, it will be possible to think in ways that are not yet open to us. These different ways of thinking will be especially useful for generating new ideas and solving problems. But by far the most important use of the new word would be to prevent the emergence of those widespread and fierce problems which are actually created by the limitations of language and mind. Even the mere existence of the new word, whether it is used or not, would help in this regard.

New words are continually being invented to describe new things. But to invent a new functional word, a new tool for thought and language, is a different matter. It has never been consciously done before in the whole history of language. What justification can there be for so presumptuous a step? What function would the word perform? Why is the word necessary?

The whole of our thinking, the whole of our language, the whole of our education, perhaps the whole of our Western culture, is concerned with the formation and communication of ideas. This is the way the brain works. This is the way the brain needs to work to make life possible. This is the way we encourage the brain to work. But what about the process of changing concepts as opposed to establishing them? This is an unnatural process for which we have no tools and no training. Until today, ideas have always lived longer than people, but now people live longer than ideas. As a result there is a great need for mental tools that make possible the re-forming of ideas.

Yet the necessity for this new word and its function does not arise from the philosophical need for it, but from the mechanics of the way the brain handles information. As a biological information-processing system the mechanical behaviour of the brain has certain limitations, and it is these limitations which make the new word so necessary and also define its function. The new word is a device for overcoming these limitations. Like the zero in mathematics, the device is a symbol and its use to carry out processes that would be impossible without it.

In the first half of the book the organization of the brain is put together. Starting with simple units, the organization is built up step by step until the mechanism of mind has been assembled. The steps are small. No special knowledge or mathematical understanding is assumed.

At the end of this first half the mechanism may be compared to a large piece of paper with writing on it. The paper is in the dark and across its surface moves a small pool of light as from a flashlight. The words illuminated by the light are read out. The words represent information stored in the brain. The first half of the book deals with how the writing comes to write itself on the paper; how it is not put there by some outside intelligence but how it comes to arrange itself to give sense and significance. How the pool of light comes to move across the paper of its own accord without there being any outside source of light or any hand to guide it. Why the light moves in one direction and not in another. How the words are not read but read themselves. Such things are the basic mechanics of consciousness, of free will, of memory and of thinking. In this first half is shown how the brain is a good computer simply because it is a bad memory. It is this bad memory that provides the computing function.

The second half of the book shows how the mechanism put together in the first half actually works in practice. The second half is concerned with why the mechanism can only work in certain ways, with the advantages and disadvantages of these ways. The inescapable limitations of thinking are examined. The four basic types of thinking are described: natural, logical, mathematical and lateral. In part these are natural and in part they are the result of artificial devices that have been developed to improve the natural behaviour of the mechanism of mind. The necessity for a new artificial device and the function of this new device are outlined.

The way the brain works does depend on the way it is put together, but there may be some readers who would prefer to accept the brain as a functioning mechanism rather than carefully follow how the organization is put together. Such readers should turn at once to Part Two, page 177. At this point the brain is like the piece of paper bearing significant patterns which are revealed in turn by the moving pool of light. These readers may return later to Part One in order to find out why the brain works in this way.

Other readers may prefer to start at the beginning and gradually work through the organization of the mechanism before proceeding to read about how it works.

Choose whichever approach you feel might suit you, but bear in mind that to most people the second part will be easier than the first. The first part deals with the beauty of function, of process and organization. The second part deals directly with how the brain thinks, how people think. The second part arises from the first as a flower arises from its stem. The purpose of the stem is to bear the flower. Without a stem only an artificial flower can survive.

Just as the unfolding of a passage of music is a matter of repetition and progression, so is the writing of this book.

Edward de Bono

At that time the gates of my Oxford college were locked at twenty minutes past midnight. Any undergraduate who wanted to get back into the place after that time did so by climbing in. On my first night I went off to a party in London, and knowing that I would be back late I asked an old hand to tell me the way to get in. It seemed quite straightforward. First there was a set of railings, and then one came to a wall which had to be climbed. Beyond the first wall there was a second wall which also had to be climbed.

It was late when I got back. The railings were easy. The first wall was rather more difficult. I got over it and went forward until I came to the second wall, which was about the same height as the first wall. I climbed this second wall, only to find myself outside again. My double effort had involved my climbing in and out across a corner.

I started again and with more careful direction came up to the proper second wall. There was an iron gate in this second wall, and as the gate was lower than the rest of the wall and also offered better footholds I climbed the gate. As I was sitting astride the top of the gate it swung open. It had never been closed.

PART I

CHAPTER 1

Systems do not have to be complicated or unintelligible, or even dressed in jargon. A system is just an arrangement of circumstances that makes things happen in a certain way. The circumstances may be metal grids, electronic components, warm bodies, rules and regulations, or anything else. In each case what actually happens is determined by the nature of the system. One can take the function of the system for granted and become interested in how it is carried out.

If young children are asked to invent a potato-peeling machine they draw a winding tube through which a string of potatoes is seen travelling towards a simple box with the explanatory note, 'In here the potatoes are peeled'. Another tube carries the peeled potatoes away. There is nothing mysterious about the box, it just performs the potato-peeling function. One takes it for granted that that is the function of the box and that somehow the function gets carried out. In some of the inventions the potatoes are then carried to a metal grid through which they are forced in order to make chips. The making of the chips is not taken for granted but explained, because it is explicable.

If you put water instead of oil into a frying pan you would not expect to be able to fry chips. If you were to use fat or oil you would get some ordinary chips. If you add a little water to the oil before you put the pan on the fire, then the temperature of the oil will rise more slowly and the chips will be soft on the inside and crisp on the outside – much more so than if only the oil had been used. The nature of the system determines what happens.

The brain is a system in which things happen according to the nature of the system. What happens in the brain is information. And the way it happens is thinking.

Since thinking in this broad sense determines what people do on any level from the most personal to the most international, it could be worth looking at some aspects of the brain system. If one were to discover all there was to know about the brain system, of what practical use would this be?

If you want to get your shoes cleaned in an English hotel you simply leave them overnight in the corridor outside your room. Many an unhappy Englishman has learned that in America shoes treated in this way disappear never to be seen again. Left outside the door, the shoes are regarded as a rather eccentric form of tipping or garbage disposal. The first useful thing that can come out of knowledge of a system is the avoiding of those errors that arise through thinking the system to be something that it is not.

The second useful thing is awareness of the limitations of the system. No matter how good they may be at performing their best functions, most systems are rather poor when it comes to performing the opposite functions. One would no more go racing in a shopping car than shopping in a racing car. Where one can, one chooses the system to fit the purpose. More often there is no choice, and this means that a single system will perform certain functions well but others not so well. For instance the brain system is well suited to developing ideas but not so good at generating them. Knowing about the limitations of a system does not by itself alter them. But by being aware of the nature of the system one can make deliberate adjustments.

The first advertisement to proclaim that a certain brand of soap was superior to all others might well have induced people to buy that soap, since they were inclined to believe what they were told. But an increasing awareness of the advertising system would cause people to make adjustments that would lessen the inevitability of the response.

The third way in which one could use knowledge of a system would be to make use of the characteristics of the system to improve its performance or to achieve some end.

In the early days of the instant breath-test for drinking drivers, one drunken driver drove his car into a lamp-post and wrecked it. As he sat waiting in the wreckage for the police to come and test and charge him, he remembered the nature of the system. So he pulled out a hip-flask and started to drink some more. When the police came he explained to them that the shock of the accident had caused him to have a drink. Since his car was no longer drivable he knew that he could not be held to have the necessary intent to drive, as required by the system. What his blood alcohol level had been at the time of the accident was, of course, no longer determinable.

Ovulation in the human female can only occur when there is the right amount of certain hormones in the body. Altering the amount of these hormones will prevent ovulation. Thus, by taking advantage of the nature of the system, effective contraception can be achieved with small doses of synthetic hormones taken by mouth in the form of a tiny pill.

In both these examples, knowledge of how a system works enables one to make effective use of it. The practice of medicine is an obvious example of this process. For that matter so is the whole of science, which tries to understand systems in order to make better use of them.

Some understanding of how the brain system handled information could be very useful. It might then be possible to recognize some of the errors and faults inherent in this type of system, to show, for example, that there was a tendency to arbitrary and self-enhancing divisions which were extremely useful in most cases but could also be the source of a lot of trouble. Apart from becoming aware of the errors of the system, it might also be possible to make more effective use of it through understanding its nature in order to make the learning process easier and more economic. It might be possible to do something about communication.

Language, notation and mathematics are useful artificial aids to thinking. There may be other artificial aids which could be invented if one had sufficient understanding of the brain system. With new notation it might prove possible to generate ideas as easily as we now develop them once they have been generated. For instance it might be possible to invent a new word which would be functional in nature like 'and', 'if', 'but' or 'not'. The function of this new word would be to compensate for the inherent limitations of the information-processing system in the brain and open up new ways of talking and thinking. The word would ultimately have to justify its usefulness in practice, but its invention may not have been possible without an understanding of the nature of the system.

Something as definite as a new word would be a very practical outcome of understanding the system. Such an understanding could also have a more general usefulness in showing that there is no inaccessible magic about the system, only an intimidating complexity.

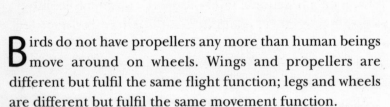

CHAPTER 2

Birds do not have propellers any more than human beings move around on wheels. Wings and propellers are different but fulfil the same flight function; legs and wheels are different but fulfil the same movement function.

Interest in the behaviour of computers as information-processing systems has aroused interest in the behaviour of the brain itself as an information-processing system. It is probable that without the computer interest there would be much less interest in the possibility of treating the brain in this way. Many useful ideas have originated in the computer field and proved useful in understanding the function of the brain. But there may be very fundamental differences in behaviour between computer systems and the brain system. In some ways, the dominance of computer ideas may actually lead away from a better understanding of brain function.

It is true that both computers and the brain work by electricity. Both England and the United States speak the same language, but this is sometimes more a cause of misunderstanding than of understanding, and it has been said that the two countries are divided by a common language. The behaviour of the electrical system in the brain is fundamentally different on several points from that to be found in computers. For instance, in a nerve circuit two single impulses starting at opposite ends of a 'wire' will cancel each other out. This is quite different from what would happen with computer electricity. The differences are so great that there is really little point in calling the two processes by the same name.

Even on a functional level there are considerable differences. For instance, computers find pattern recognition, such as the recognition of a hand-written letter of the alphabet, very difficult, but complicated sequences of mathematical operations very easy. The brain system on the other hand finds pattern recognition easier than anything else, but has great difficulty with sequences of mathematical operations.

Computers have dull and exact memories. Material is stored away in the memory and then brought out again later, exactly as it went in. There is a processing part of the computer which does the work and a memory part which does no work but just stores things. The brain system is probably quite different. There may be no special computing part at all – only a rather poor memory. Paradoxically, because it is a poor memory it may function as an excellent computer. It is a poor memory because it does not simply store the information that it receives, but picks and chooses and alters the information. This is processing behaviour, so what comes out of the memory is very unlikely to be the same as what went in.

Laughter is a fundamental characteristic of the brain system but not of the computer system. And with laughter goes creativity. It will be a sinister day when computers start to laugh, because that will mean they are capable of a lot of other things as well.

It is perfectly possible that a computer could be deliberately programmed to imitate the functions of the brain system, probably even to the extent of laughter and creativity. But this would not mean that the two systems were functioning in a similar manner except on the final level, that is to say the outcome level. It is quite easy to tell someone to draw a square, but much more cumbersome to give him the mathematical definition of a square, though the outcome would be the same. A similarity of outcome does not imply a similarity of process.

SIMPLICITY AND COMPLEXITY

When one looks at a complex structure it is very difficult to imagine that it could have been assembled out of simple units. When one considers a complex operation it is very difficult to imagine that it is made up from the interaction of simple processes. Even if one is ready to accept such possibilities it is still difficult to see how the units or operations come together.

On page 19 is an apparently complicated pattern. What is the basic principle of organization of this pattern?

On page 20 are shown four outline figures. Each of these figures is assembled out of the same type of basic unit. What are these units and how do they fit together?

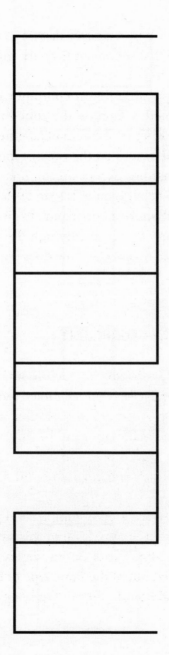

Fig. 1

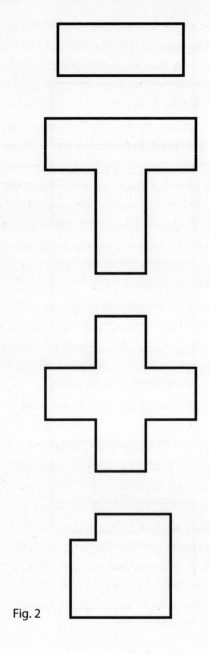

Fig. 2

The brain appears to be such an immensely complicated system that it would seem to require a very complicated explanation. But even the most complicated processes may be based on simple ones. The most complicated mathematical processes ultimately depend on the four basic processes of addition, subtraction, multiplication and division that a schoolboy learns at school. Yet it is a far cry from school copybooks to working out the mathematics required to land a space capsule accurately on the moon. The most elaborate computers can solve any mathematical problem by using even fewer basic processes. Ultimately the whole business of computing rests on the simple process whereby a switch can change from one state to one other state, from on to off or the other way round. Millions of such switches arranged in different ways, in space or time, are the basis of computing.

The elaboration of a few basic principles gives rise to the richest musical symphony. The elaboration of a few basic principles in physics explains much of the universe. The simple basic process of evolution by random mutation and survival of the fittest ultimately leads to a complicated variety of species.

When one starts from the simple basic units it is easy to see how they can be built up into complicated structures capable of complicated functions. But when one starts from the complicated structures or functions then it is not so easy to see the basic processes. In this book the intention is not to break down the complicated behaviour of the brain system into simple basic processes, but to show that simple basic processes can be put together to give a system that is capable of as complicated behaviour as the brain system.

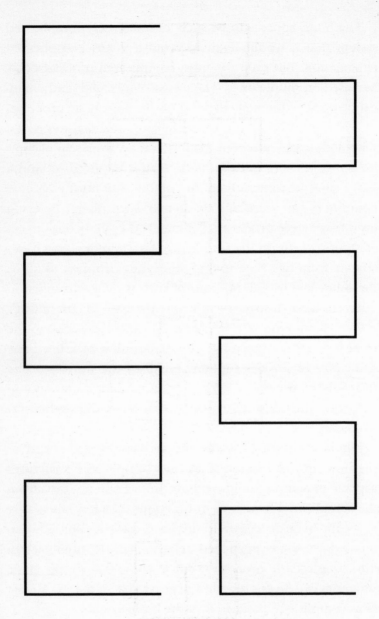

Fig. 3

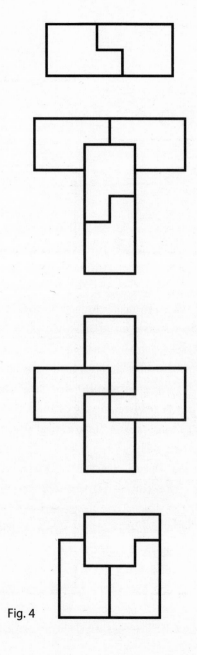

Fig. 4

CHAPTER 3

The building of houses is a complicated business. There is the man who understands the chemical composition of bricks and the best material to make them from. The next man thoroughly understands the brick-making process and makes full use of the material selected by the first man, even though he does not know much about that material. Then there is the bricklayer, who handles and lays the bricks. The foreman organizes the bricklayers, and tells them where to lay the bricks, but is not very good at laying them himself. The contractor organizes the supply of materials and labour and sees that the job gets done. The actual shape and design of the house is arranged by the architect, who may not know too much about the details that have gone before. At the next level comes the town-planner who decides how to distribute the houses. Above the town-planner may come the over-all planner, who decides where the new towns must go with reference to transport systems, population distribution and the changing economics of different areas.

In the process there are eight levels of organization. At each level the output of the level below is taken as a unit and organized as such. The detailed organization of the unit itself is not required, it is taken for granted and dealt with as a whole. For the bricklayer the functional unit is a brick. For the contractor the units are labour, bricks and transport, which all have to be co-ordinated. For the town-planner it is complete house units.

If one were to understand fully the chemical processes involved in the making of a brick this would not give much insight into the architect's design of the house or the town-planner's distribution of the houses. At some point the actual nature of the brick does come into consideration at these other levels. For instance if the bricks were extremely heavy then the contractor would have to take account of this in his use of labour and transport.

Some knowledge of the properties of the basic unit is required at each level, but a detailed knowledge of the basic unit does not itself give any information about the higher levels of organization. The higher the level of organization the less relevant is detailed knowledge of the basic unit, provided its properties are consistent with the way it is being used. Thus the over-all planner may not really care whether the houses are built of bricks or concrete.

The triode valve and the transistor perform roughly the same function, though their structure is very different, and it is the function of the device and not its detailed structure that matters for computers. It is true that complete ignorance of the difference in size between the triode valve and the transistor could lead to the design of impossibly bulky equipment, and ignorance of the heat sensitivity of transistors could also lead to design trouble. But what really matters is the understanding of the basic function of the unit in broad terms. Increasingly detailed knowledge about the triode valve or transistor will not of itself give any information about the higher level of organization of the units into a computing system.

Just as detailed information at the most basic level of organization may never tell anything about the higher levels of organization, so information at the higher levels of organization can be useful even if the detailed information is not available. A politician may make practical decisions concerning the use of nuclear explosives even though he does not understand the detailed physical processes involved. What he needs to know is the availability of the devices, the possibility of delivering them to the site of destruction and an estimate of the degree of destruction in both immediate and long-term effects.

With regard to the brain system certain broad functions of nerve cell units are known. More detailed knowledge at this level will not necessarily reveal anything about the higher level of organization of the units. Equally, certain broad principles of organization at the higher levels may not await more detailed knowledge of the basic units. In terms of the over-all organization, once the function of a unit is clear it does not matter by exactly what mechanism the function is carried out.

The difficulty lies in deciding at what level of organization it is best to explore the functioning of a system. If the level is too detailed and the units are too small, then the over-all function of the system may not be disclosed at all. On the other hand if the level is too high one may only be able to describe the system in broad functional terms that are of no practical use whatsoever. For instance, one may come to the conclusion that the brain processes information, or that it can recognize patterns. Ideally one would like to choose a level of explanation that not only explained observations adequately but also allowed one to make useful predictions.

The degree of usefulness of a prediction does not have to be absolute. It may only be possible to predict a certain type of behaviour, and not the detailed behaviour itself. Yet this can still be useful. It is certainly a good deal better than nothing.

Consider the system of a man sitting down at a table and shaking a die in his hands. Now and again he throws the die onto the table. From this broad description of the system you cannot tell which number is going to come up, or at what time it is going to come up. But even from this description you can still tell quite a lot. You can be sure that no number greater than six will come up. You can also be sure that if the process continues long enough each number from one to six will appear about as often as any other. It might be much more useful if you could tell exactly when a particular number would come up, but to fall short of such detailed description does not mean that one cannot predict anything useful, such as an even distribution.

Two men start out at the same time on journeys from two separate places. That is the first level of description of the system. They set out from different points along the same road and travel towards each other. This is the second level of description, and even at this level one can predict something useful. Somewhere, sometime, they must meet, no matter how fast they travel or how far apart their starting-points may have been. The third level of description is to know that the starting-points are 30 miles apart, that A starts at 8 a.m. and travels at 6 m.p.h., that B starts at 10 a.m. and travels at

4 m.p.h. From this information one can predict that they will meet at 11.48 a.m. at 7.2 miles from the starting place of B. At first sight this detailed prediction may appear to be much more use than the simple prediction that they would meet somewhere. But it may not actually be all that much more useful. Perhaps the important thing was that the two should never meet since they were sworn enemies. In that case it would have been better to make the simple prediction at once rather than to refuse to make any prediction until more detailed information was available.

CHAPTER 4

Philosophical word descriptions can never be wrong, for what is described has been created by the process of description. Words like 'self', 'consciousness', 'free will', 'humour', 'motivation', 'learning' and 'insight' are useful as catalogue descriptions for the purpose of communication, but useless as explanations. They create themselves in a manner that has its own consistency but does not explain what is being described.

'Suicide is caused by the self-destructive tendencies inherent in mankind.' At first sight this sentence seems to offer a useful explanation of the phenomenon of suicide. But does it? Suicide is clearly self-destruction, and one can use the latter phrase instead of the word. When members of a species do actually commit suicide then it is fair to say that there is a suicidal tendency in that species. Since the species in question is mankind, the tendencies are inherent in mankind. Thus the sentence, 'Suicide is caused by self-destructive tendencies inherent in mankind', explains no more than a sentence which reads, 'Suicide is accounted for by the fact that people do actually commit suicide'.

As explanation, the sentence offers nothing except tail-chasing, but as description it does have a value. It suggests that suicide may not be an abnormal aberration, or due to external pressures, but the expression of an inclination which is part of the make-up of mankind. That may be so, but as mere description one is not entitled to build on it as if it were some real phenomenon. Otherwise one just ends up with words chasing words into a pattern of great intricacy and little use.

The sort of mess one can get into with words is shown by some of the old arguments about determinism, free will, responsibility and punishment. The argument is that if a person's actions are entirely determined then he is no longer responsible for them, and hence it is unjust to punish him. One might equally well argue that the only possible justification for punishment was that the actions were determined. One would hope that the memory or anticipation of punishment would become one of the determining factors. It all depends where one draws the boundary for self: whether self includes the determining factors or is supposed to stand apart from them.

In order to make any progress one tries to get away from words as things in themselves and tries to use them only as descriptions of other things which exist in their own right. If the behaviour of a car is determined by its design and the power of its engine, then a description of the system still involves words but they rest on the car system and not on each other.

MODELS

If you use a child's construction set to make a working model of a crane, then the way the crane works will depend on the pieces that have been chosen and how they have been put together. Once the pieces have been chosen and put together then the model will work according to its nature. The creator no longer controls but only watches it. Usually the model will behave as expected, but it can also go beyond what the creator expects. Once it has been constructed the model has a life and working of its own. If instead of actually constructing a crane you had just imagined one then you would have been free to imagine all sorts of behaviour for this crane, but this behaviour would never have taught you anything since you would be supplying it all. With a model, however, you only put the pieces together and then learn from what happens.

A model is a method of transferring some relationship or process from its actual setting to a setting where it is more conveniently studied. In a model, relationships and processes are preserved unchanged, though the things that are being related may be changed. In order to study the proportions of Westminster Abbey one might take a photograph and then study this. The photograph is a model of the abbey, and the relationships are preserved, even though it is now differently shaded areas of paper that are related. A better model would be a three-dimensional one made of wood or cardboard which would preserve even more of the relationships.

All models involve this transformation of relationships from their original setting into another. A map is the transformation of the relationships of the countryside into relationships on a piece of paper that is much more convenient to study. Once the transformation has been made then the relationships within the model itself indicate what can happen. The paths of sub-atomic particles in physics are transformed into lines of minute bubbles which can be photographed and measured. A watch is a method of transforming time into the position of one bit of metal relative to another. All scientific measuring instruments are just methods of transforming some phenomenon into something else that is easy to handle, be it a curve on a piece of paper, a pointer on a dial, or a printed figure. A book is a transformation of ideas into a black and white pattern of some permanence. Money is the transformation of work into pieces of paper.

All these transformations result in the setting up of models which represent processes or relationships in ways that are more easy to handle and examine. For instance, a temperature-recording device may transform the fluctuations in temperature in a warehouse into a wavy line on a piece of paper. Here the transformation of time into space is most convenient since it makes all the information available at a glance.

Some working models may actually carry out processes which can be examined. Other models merely represent the relationships, and the observer has to do the work. The line which represents the projection of a cone onto a piece of paper is just a line, but working from it the observer elicits the mathematics of conic sections.

A child making a model house might cut the whole thing out of cardboard or out of a cardboard box. Alternatively he could use those ready-made plastic building blocks. These blocks can be used to build any shape of building. All one has to do is to fit them together in their special way and then one can proceed to make any design one likes.

So it is with other models. One can make a special model to fit the situation, or one can make use of multipurpose model-building kits. Mathematics is the most obvious of such kits. There are pieces which fit together in certain ways and these ways are the rules of mathematics. Using the standard pieces one can represent a real-life situation by means of a model. Once the transformation has been done then the model is allowed to work according to its own rules. One follows along and sees what happens, and then translates this back into the real world to see what would have happened there. Mathematics is no more than a pencil-and-paper model-building system worked with certain rules.

NOTATION

Any notational system is a model-building system. Mathematics happens to be a system of notation with which there has been a huge amount of experience. This means that people have become very good at recognizing particular types of models and knowing exactly how to work them. Ordinary language is another notational system with its own working rules.

Because notation seems so arbitrary, it is often difficult to appreciate just how important it may be in the development of ideas. It is rather like the design of a child's building blocks. If the design is good then there is great flexibility in what can be built. A cumbersome design may make progress impossible.

The development of mathematics was held up for a long time by the cumbersome notation of the Greeks and then the Romans. The Roman system was good for adding, subtracting and tallying, but very awkward for multiplication or division. Then came the Arabic system, with its emphasis on the position of a symbol as well as its shape. Then there was the invention of the zero, which has had an immense usefulness in the development of mathematics. The invention of the decimal notation again made things easier.

Descartes's invention of co-ordinates made possible the development of analytical geometry. Newton and Leibniz independently discovered the calculus, but Newton's notation was so very cumbersome compared to that of Leibniz, that those who followed Leibniz made much more progress. This is surprising when one realizes that the basic principles were the same in each case and only the notation was different.

The effect the different types of notation have had on the development of mathematics is very striking. With the notation of language the effect is probably also very large, but it is less obvious. Choice of a convenient notation may have made possible the development of different ideas. A more important effect is the way choice of notation can make a great deal of difference to communication. It is also possible that the more complicated the notation the longer it takes to learn, and hence the more prolonged education must be. When one compares the twenty-six-letter alphabet to the huge number of Chinese characters one can appreciate the huge difference in convenience, for instance on a typewriter.

Symbolic logic is a further notational development of language that brings it closer to mathematics. It is possible that the notation of language, both as regards visual and auditory notation, may be developed further. For instance there does not yet seem to be in language an equivalent of the zero in mathematics.

Notation is quite arbitrary and quite passive. Notation may even seem insignificant beside the subject being described, just as the choice of a particular language may seem to be much less important than what is being said in that language. Yet notation is immensely important. Notation and its rules form a model in themselves, and it is the fluency of this model that determines how well the real-life situation can be explored. One would hardly set out to explore the intricacies of flight with a model aeroplane made of clay.

MODELS AND NOTATION IN THIS BOOK

In this book the function of the brain system is not described with words but with working models. The models are set up to imitate certain processes, and then one observes how they function. One watches what happens when various processes and relationships are put together. There is no question of words chasing words, creating and justifying each other in an endlessly circular fashion. Words are only used to describe the behaviour of the model, and this is independent of the words used.

The models are simple functional ones which embody basic processes that are easy to follow. It is true that many of the relationships and processes shown by these models could be just as easily shown by mathematical models, but except to those who work with them all the time mathematical models can be difficult to follow, whereas a model which makes use of the behaviour of an ordinary fruit jelly is much more accessible. The process itself may be just as subtly described by the one as by the other. The advantage of having an accessible model is that the reader can visualize it and play around with it in his mind.

In so far as mathematics is the handling of relationships, the physical models are mathematical models if they obey certain defined rules. Mathematics in its proper sense is not just the arrangement of symbols on paper. Stonehenge is a mathematical model, and so probably are the pyramids.

The advantages of using a model that can be actually played with or visualized are great when compared with mere description. A description only uses one particular way of looking at something; it describes what is noticed at the moment, what makes sense at the moment. A physical model, however, contains all that could be noticed at any time; it includes all the possible ways of looking at the situation. Should the point of view change, one can go back and find the new point of view.

On page 37 is shown a simple physical figure that could be described as an 'L' shape. This is an adequate description, but it is much less use than having the actual figure. With the actual figure one can go back again and again, paying attention now to the length of the limbs, now to the width of the limbs, now to the orientation of the figure. It is true that all these things could be included in an elaborate description, but that would be tedious. It is much better to have them stored in an accessible model so that one can have them only when one needs them.

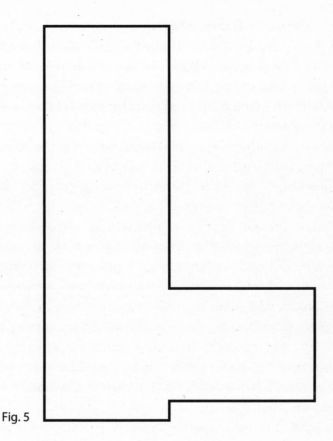

Fig. 5

Some new notations are introduced in this book. These notations have been invented to ease the business of describing certain processes and relationships which it would otherwise be awkward to describe. Like all new notations they may take some getting used to, but once one gets to know them they do make things easier.

THE MODEL AND THE BRAIN

Imitation of behaviour does not imply similarity of the mechanism underlying that behaviour. The behaviour of the information-processing system described in this book may resemble that of the brain, but this does not prove that there must be a similar mechanism acting in the brain. Nevertheless there are several reasons why such an approach may be useful.

1. The information-processing mechanism described may be of interest in itself, as an example of a self-educating and self-organizing passive system that is capable of effective information-processing by means of a few basic operations.

2. The system described is capable of such processes as 'self', 'direction of attention', 'thinking', 'learning' and even 'humour'. These and other related processes are usually regarded as being specifically human in nature. That they can be imitated by a mere mechanical machine – and a passive one at that – must affect the notion that the human brain functions in some unique and magical fashion.

3. Although the system is basically very efficient, there are certain inherent faults and limitations which lead to definite types of error in the processing of information. Such inescapable errors permeate the thinking processes in the system. The idea that there may be inbuilt errors in an information-processing system may have a relevance to human thinking, even if the system itself does not.

4. Instead of the more usual verbal philosophizing as to what goes on in the mind, the system offers a mechanical philosophy. In its own right this is just as valid as the verbal descriptions, and it also avoids some of the circular tendencies of verbal descriptions. Like any myth, this mechanical one can have a useful consistency as an organizing idea, whether or not its truth can be checked.

5. By far the most important function of the system described is to throw up definite ideas which can then be examined for their own sake. The validity of the ideas is not proved by the way they come about, but once they have come about then they might prove to be valid in themselves. In this capacity the system acts as a method of generating ideas which can then survive on their own.

6. Even though no formal attempt is made to prove that the information-processing system described is the one operating in the brain, there is evidence to suggest that it may be. The actual details of the system may be different, but the broad class of system is probably the same. In a later section the resemblance between the functional units used in the information-processing system and those operating in the brain is discussed.

Whatever else it does, the description of the information-processing system ought to stimulate the reader's own ideas about the dependence of brain function on its structure.

One talks of a computer having a memory. This is using a human analogy to describe a mechanical process. In the course of this book the processes that occur in the model are often described as if they were occurring in the human brain. This is carrying the same analogy process further, for it would be quite impossible to describe the processes in other terms. It is not meant to be a back-door way of implying that similarity of behaviour proves similarity of mechanism.

CHAPTER 5

MEMORY

A memory is what is left behind when something happens and does not completely unhappen. This trace does not have to be in a special place, and it does not have to tell much about what has happened.

If you walk through a swing door and it swings to behind you there is no memory of what has happened. If you walk through an ordinary door and leave it open behind you then the open door is a memory of your passage. The door is not the same as it was before – as other people in the room will be quick to point out.

If a dog walks across the carpet and out of the room there is no memory of its presence except to sensitive nostrils. If the dog had had muddy paws then the memory-trace would be more obvious.

It may be that in Indian restaurants the plates are made deliberately small in order to make the portions seem bigger, or it may be that the portions really are big, for you do not have to be a particularly messy eater to leave curry stains on the table-cloth. The curry stains are a memory. Anything that remains after the action causing it has ceased is a memory of the action.

The curry stains on the table-cloth are an example of the most familiar form of memory, that is, marks upon a surface. Writing, drawing or photographs are all instances of this type of memory-trace.

From a door which has been left open, from muddy marks on the carpet, from curry stains on the table-cloth, one cannot tell much about what has happened. The door may have been opened by the wind. The marks on the carpet may have been made by a cat or may even be a modern interior-decorating joke. The curry stains may have been made by a chimpanzee. This does not stop the open door, the muddy marks and the curry stains from being memories, for a memory does not have to be particularly informative about what has caused it. The interpretation or read-back of the memory may be difficult, misleading or even impossible. But as long as there is something to try and read back then there is a memory.

A photograph is an arrangement of silver particles on a piece of paper. The arrangement forms a memory of what-ever was photographed. Usually a photograph is a good memory-trace and is not difficult to interpret. Even so, the interpretation of photographs does require experience. If photographs are shown to primitive people who have never seen any pictorial representation, then they are quite unable to make anything of the blobs of light and shade that make up a photograph.

A perfect memory-trace is one which requires no effort of interpretation at all. This is because the memory actually recreates the event which caused it. A good example is the recording of sounds. This recording process converts patterns in time into patterns in space. Patterns in time would be impossible to store; patterns in space are very easy to store. Apart from the pattern, there is no physical resemblance between a sound and the arrangement of tiny bumps on a plastic disc or the distribution of magnetization along a tape. Yet a gramophone or a tape-recorder will convert these arrangements back into the actual sound that produced them. No memory system could be more perfect.

When one is short of perfection one is guessing at what might have happened from what has been left behind. With a reasonable photograph one does not have to be very good at guessing. With the open door, the muddy marks on the carpet, the curry stains on the table-cloth, one has to guess rather harder.

Experience makes guessing easier, and so do other clues. Your knowledge of the door catch and its usual behaviour would probably exclude the likelihood of its having been opened by the wind. Your knowledge of restaurants and the scarcity of chimpanzees would make you guess that it was more likely to have been a person eating the curry even if the table-manners were not all that different. The muddy stains on the carpet arranged in certain groupings would suggest an animal. If you were to find another sort of mess in the corner the interpretation of the marks would be that much easier. And if you had some experience in tracking you might be able to distinguish a cat's prints from a dog's. In each case, things quite apart from the memory-trace itself make it easier and easier to read back.

Thus a memory-trace does not have to be particularly informative in itself in order to be useful. It may be useless on its own, but very useful when fitted into a general picture – as the great detective writers show all the time. It is enough that a memory is what is left behind when something happens and does not completely unhappen.

LESS OBVIOUS MEMORIES

One usually thinks of memories as being recorded on blank sheets, just as a fresh piece of film is used for a new photograph. That sort of memory is easy to notice. But a memory may only alter something that is going on anyway.

A painter is painting a portrait. His child jogs his elbow. What happens on the canvas is a memory of that jog. The result may be an obvious squiggle or it may be no more than an alteration in the shape of one of the ears in the portrait. It would be easy to notice the squiggle and try and interpret it. The alteration in the shape of the ear is just as real a memory but much more difficult to interpret. Yet most memories are modifications in a process that is going on already rather than marks set apart by themselves.

Another sort of memory is even less obvious. One does not always expect a memory to play back the events of which it is a record, but one does expect a memory to give some indication of these events. There are, however, memories which do not have a tangible form that can be examined. Such memories simply make it easier for something that has happened to happen again.

If you were to dislocate your shoulder there might be nothing to show for it after it had healed up. Nor would an X-ray show anything. Nevertheless, it would be slightly easier for the shoulder to be dislocated again. A second dislocation would make a third one more likely, and so on. Memory of the dislocations would accumulate as an increasing tendency to dislocation until in the end you might have to have an operation which would really put it right. This facilitating effect is a hidden memory which is not manifest as itself but only as a tendency for something that has happened to happen again.

In a way this facilitating memory is an active memory, for instead of just being a passive indication of what has happened it actually helps to re-create the event.

A simple model of this type of memory can be made with children's building blocks of the plastic snap-together variety. Some of these blocks are fitted together to make small columns which are stood on a board as shown in the picture on page 46. If you gradually tilt the board by lifting up one end then there will come a point when one or more of the columns will topple over. Since this is an artificial model one can now add an artificial rule of behaviour. This special rule decrees that each time a column topples over another block is added on to that column to make it taller. The columns are then stood up again and the tilting repeated. This time some of the columns are taller than the others and it is these taller columns which will topple over first. So you add more blocks to these columns and that makes them taller still and even more likely to topple over. The short columns, on the other hand, get less and less chance to topple over, for the tall columns now topple over when the board has hardly been tilted at all. According to the rules of this model, something that happens makes it easier for that thing to happen again. There are other very interesting principles illustrated in this model, but they will be discussed later.

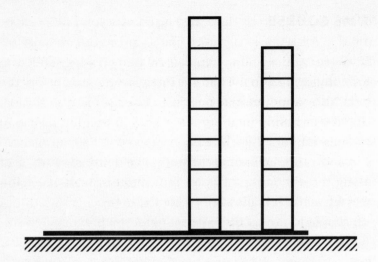

Fig. 6

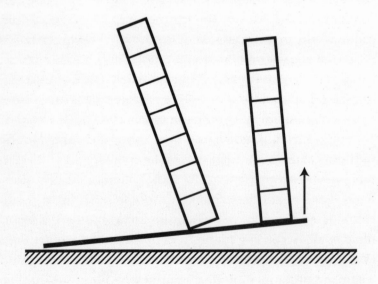

Fig. 7

TIME COURSE

If you eat a sticky bun, your fingers remain sticky after you have finished eating. That is a short-lasting memory of the bun. Your appetite may be satisfied for some hours. That is a longer-lasting memory. Your gain in weight may be all too permanent.

A short-term memory is but a small extension of an event along the dimension of time. Yet even this small extension may be useful if it allows the interaction between two things which would otherwise have been quite separate.

Footprints in the sand on the edge of the sea fade pretty quickly. If you were late for a holiday rendezvous on the beach and when you got there the beach was empty, you would not be able to tell whether the girl had come and gone or never come at all. But if there were footprints on the sand by the edge of the sea then you would know, and perhaps even how long she had waited. A summer tan is another short-term memory that fades all too quickly. Even so, a girl returning from holiday beautiful with tan may attract the attention of an admirer who becomes a long-term event. A short-term memory is just a way of extending the influence of an event beyond the real time of its occurrence.

PLAY-BACK

What we really require of a memory-trace is that it should tell us what happened, what caused it. Where possible, we actually force the memory-trace to re-create the event of which it is a memory. We attack the gramophone record with the pick-up head in order to make it re-create for our amusement the sounds that it holds as a memory arranged in patterns of plastic bumps. It is a selfish need on our part because we are standing outside the record.

If the gramophone record had a soul and consciousness it would not bother about playing out the music. The pattern of bumps would itself re-create the music without any need to play it out. The soul of the record would only become conscious of the music as the bumps formed in the first place. This would be its sole reaction to the music. Once the bumps had been formed, then going over them again would re-create the music, and the record could mutter to itself, 'Ah yes, this is Beethoven's Fifth', or, 'This is the Beatles', as it recognized the different pattern of bumps. But because we have no regard for the 'consciousness' of the record we use it as a passive source of our pleasure.

A friend who has come back from an interesting trip abroad is pumped with questions and required to play back the experiences for our benefit. As far as the friend is concerned his memory of the events does not depend on the sound he makes when he talks about them.

If a table-cloth were a consciousness surface then the curry stains would be that table-cloth's way of being aware of what was happening above it. It would be a limited sort of consciousness, capable of only a few perceptions: nothing happening, small curry stains, large curry stains, curry stains in several different areas. Yet the pattern would be repeatable. Whenever a curry stain appeared on the table-cloth its consciousness would recognize a curry-stain-producing situation. If a fake curry stain were produced then the table-cloth would mistakenly identify the situation as a curry-stain-producing one.

Memories constitute their own consciousness and their own perception. There is no need to play back to something outside of themselves.

A blind man may know that a certain person is in the room by the sound of that person's voice. If that same pattern of sound could be produced in another way (for instance by a very good tape-recorder) then the blind man would know that the person was in the room even when he was not. He would not just think it but actually know it, since what he received would be the same in each case.

The total reaction of a photographic plate to a camel which is photographed onto it is the pattern of light and shade upon its surface. If exactly the same pattern could be produced in some other way than by having a camel present, then as far as the plate was concerned there would be no difference. If the appropriate pattern of light and shade were copied from another photograph, the plate would still have the complete camel experience. If the pattern on the plate gradually changed from some other image to the camel image, then the plate would suddenly come to have the camel experience.

If an event causes a particular pattern to form on a memory-surface, then reactivation of that same pattern will re-create the event as far as the memory-surface is concerned. One can forget about the need for play-back and the need for some outside agent to make use of what is on a memory-surface.

STORING MEMORIES

Different memories are different patterns left behind by different things. If one wants to be able to recognize the different things, then the memory-traces must be kept separate from each other in such a way that they can be made use of on their own. What sort of system would one need in order to store thousands and thousands of different memory-traces? Each memory-trace is a unique pattern on the memory-surface. How large a surface would one need to store so many patterns?

On page 51 is shown a single box. With such a box you can represent two patterns: the box with a cross in it and the box without a cross. If you had two boxes you could have four different patterns. If you had three boxes you could have eight different patterns. Each time you add a box you double the number of patterns that can be shown. With nine boxes (as in a noughts-and-crosses grid) the total number of different patterns would be 512. That means that there are 512 distinguishable ways of distributing crosses over the nine boxes.

If you had a grid made up of ten boxes along one side and ten along the other, then the total number of different patterns that could be shown would be about 10,000,000,000, 000,000,000,000,000,000. In visual terms that would mean that if each pattern were given a separate name, and a thousand such names were written on each piece of paper, and these pieces of paper were piled up, then they would reach to the moon – and back. Not once but several million times. That is the size of the number of patterns which could be represented in this manner with just 100 units. In the brain there are of the order of a trillion units.

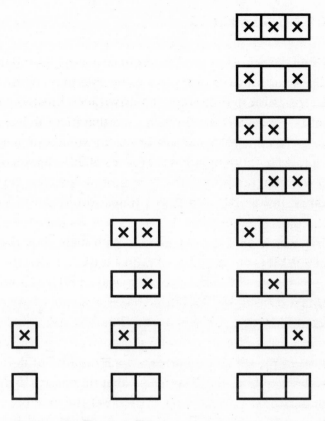

Fig. 8

Suppose a grid of fine lines transferred to the surface of a photographic plate. Suppose that each of the grid boxes on the surface of the plate was classified as either light or dark (in-between shades would be judged as either one or the other) according to how the photograph had come out. Then by specifying the state of each box one could recognize several billion different objects, provided they were always photographed from the same point of view and distance.

That is, provided the image fell on the same part of the plate. If a camel were photographed there would be on the plate a certain pattern of light and dark boxes which would make up the image of the camel. The same would be true for any other image on the photographic plate. Each picture image could be described as a pattern of light or dark boxes. If there are a sufficient number of separate, identifiable boxes on the surface then a vast number of different patterns can be received.

But all this is no more than a long-winded way of saying that a photograph may be taken of a vast number of things, each of which will give a distinct image. Any photograph can be imagined to be made up of tiny boxes or not, without its capacity for receiving images being altered. The box idea is really a way of showing that any surface capable of receiving a recognizable image pattern is capable of receiving a multitude of such patterns.

Dividing the surface of the photograph into boxes does not make it capable of receiving more images, but it is a convenient device for considering what happens at each point on the surface. Any memory-surface that is capable of registering an impression may be considered as being made up of boxes or dots or units. It is enough that each of these units should be capable of change. The minimum requirement for change is that there should be two states which can be distinguished one from the other. These two states might be a cross or no cross, as in the grid pattern, dark or light, as in the photograph boxes, on or off, as with a switch or light bulb.

As soon as there are a sufficient number of such units, each capable of being in one of two states (that is to say capable of change), then there is a surface which can record a huge number of distinct patterns, just as an ordinary photographic plate can.

How the patterns are stored as separate memories will be considered later. It is for convenience in describing this process that the surface is divided into individual units. For the convenience of one's imagination the units are considered to be spread over a flat surface. Such a flat surface, made up of units each of which is capable of indicating a change, can be called a memory-surface.

FUNCTIONAL CONNECTIONS

Each unit on the memory-surface has a special position, and if the units were lights then a picture would be given if the units in specified positions lit up. In two-dimensional space the position of each unit is given by its relationship to the neighbours which surround it.

It is this fixed relationship in space that allows the memory-surface to record and keep images. If the units kept wandering about after the image had been received then the image would literally go to pieces.

Any one unit is most closely related to the units which are nearest to it in space. Instead of nearness in space one could substitute nearness in sympathy. Nearness in sympathy is another way of saying functional connection.

If you go with your friends to a football match but get split up by the rush of the crowd, you might find yourself standing on your own. The people around you are your neighbours in space, but your friends scattered throughout the crowd are nearest to you in sympathy.

When you use an underground station in London you are surrounded by masses of people who are your neighbours in space. Yet each one of those people is functionally connected to a completely different set of people who are not at that moment spatial neighbours at all. The functional connection of these people is a communication one. They are not actually connected by wires all the time but they are connected by the functional equivalent of communication wires, that is to say, knowledge of telephone numbers, addresses, names, familiarity.

On the flat photographic surface each unit has a spatial neighbour. In the underground station or the football crowd each unit has functional neighbours who differ from the spatial neighbours.

Take nine points as shown in a simple pattern – (a) on page 55 – and then for these nine points use nine solid objects like cups. You now connect elastic bands to the handles of the cups as shown. The elastic bands represent lines of communication or a functional relationship. For the moment this functional relationship is exactly the same as the spatial one. Next jumble the cups up as much as you like. The elastic stretches and the positions alter – (b) also on page 55. The spatial relationships are all upset. But the functional relationships are exactly the same.

Suppose you started off the other way round with the jumbled mess, but then sorted it out so that the functional relationships coincided with the spatial ones. You could then forget about the functional relationships and deal only with the much more convenient spatial ones.

Throughout this book all the models and descriptions refer to the memory-surface as a flat one with spatial relationships.

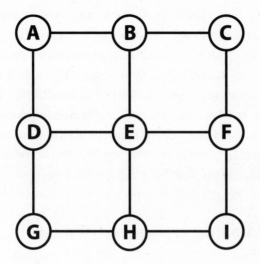

Fig. 9a

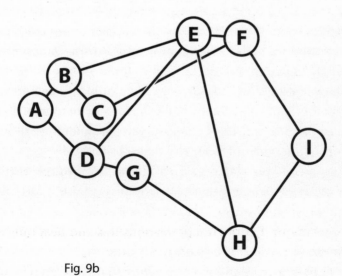

Fig. 9b

Everything that is said in this context can be applied just as well to functional relationships. And by functional relationships is simply meant a communication line. And by communication line is simply meant sympathy, so that when something happens at one unit any other functionally connected unit will feel something of that happening.

We can now forget about functional relationships and go back to memory-surfaces with simple spatial relationships, in which each unit is related to its neighbours.

GOOD AND BAD MEMORY-SURFACES

When you take a photograph you expect to get a good picture, to find on the film a true representation of whatever you have photographed. Suppose you came back from a trip abroad and found that there had been something wrong with the film in your camera; the film had been wrinkled in some way and this wrinkling had distorted all your pictures. Or there was something wrong with the emulsion on the film and only part of each photograph had come out. You would be very annoyed. A photographic film is expected to be a good memory-surface. Up to this point it has been assumed that memory-surfaces are good memory-surfaces, and that they faithfully record the image as it is presented to them. It has been supposed that the memory-surfaces are passive and just receive images in a neutral fashion without altering the image.

The wrinkled or blotchy film, however, is a different sort of memory-surface. It is a memory-surface with characteristics of its own which result in an alteration of the received image, so that it is no longer pure and exact.

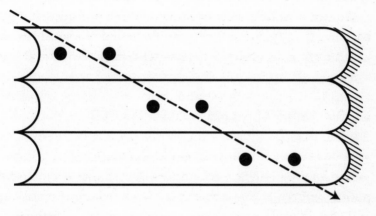

Fig. 10a

Fig. 10b

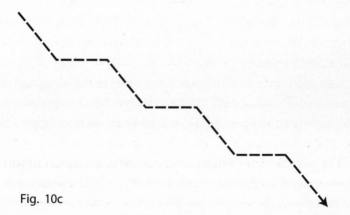

Fig. 10c

If you walk across a patch of sand and drop marbles at one-second intervals, these marbles will come to form a pattern on the sand. The sand acts as a memory-surface, and the dropped marbles are the memory-trace. From this memory-trace one could tell the direction of your walk and also its speed (from the distance apart of the marbles). The pattern that might result is shown in picture (a) on page 57. Now suppose that instead of the sand there was a special corrugated surface, as shown in cross-section in picture (b). If you were to walk across this corrugated surface at an angle (as shown by the dotted line) and drop the marbles as before, a rather different pattern would result. Neither your walk nor the way you dropped the marbles is any different from what it had been before. The difference in pattern is due to the memory-surface which has done something to the marbles instead of just accepting them where they fell. It has altered the pattern presented to it and comes to show something rather different. This is rather like the wretched film that spoiled the holiday photographs. If you did not know anything about the nature of the corrugated surface and just looked at the position of the marbles, you might suppose that the path of the walk had been zig-zag instead of straight – picture (c).

Suppose the surface was neither sand nor corrugated, but concrete. The dropped marbles would then jump about and roll all over the place in a random manner from which one would not be able to tell anything about the walk.

On page 59 are shown the patterns that would result in all three cases. The first pattern is made by a true memory-surface. The second pattern is made by a memory-surface which does something to the material received. The third pattern

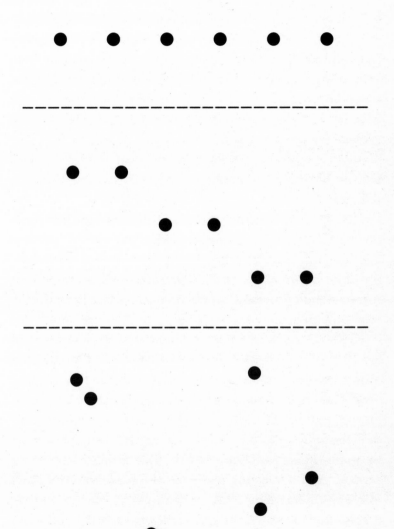

Fig. 11

is also made by a memory-surface which does something to the material received, but in a completely random manner.

A good memory-surface gives back exactly what has been put onto that surface. A bad memory-surface gives back something different. The difference between what is put onto the surface and what is given back (or stays there) is what the memory-surface does to the material. The material is changed and processed by the memory-surface. This processing is not necessarily an active or a worthwhile business, but just the way a bad memory-surface works even when it is trying to do its best.

The extraordinary thing is that a bad memory-surface can be more useful than a good memory-surface when it comes to handling information. A good memory-surface does nothing but store information, and a separate system is required to sort it out and process it. A bad memory-surface actually processes the material itself and so is a complete computer.

The two ways in which a bad memory-surface can be bad are distortion and incompleteness. Distortion means that things are shoved around, emphasis is changed, relationships may be altered. Incompleteness means that some things are just left out. Paradoxically, this is a tremendously important deficiency, for when some things are left out there must be some things which are left in. This implies a selecting process. And a selecting process is the most powerful of all information-handling tools.

It is quite likely that the great efficiency of the brain is not due to its being a brilliant computer. The efficiency of the brain is probably due to its being a bad memory-surface. One could almost say that the function of mind is mistake.

CHAPTER 6

What happens to the information that is put onto a bad memory-surface is determined by the nature of that surface. By 'nature of the surface' is meant all the processes and rules of behaviour which taken together constitute a special universe.

A universe is a situation with special rules of its own. Anything that happens in that situation has to happen according to these rules, which are not arbitrary but arise from the way the situation is organized, from the nature of the situation.

A game of Monopoly is a universe in which quite complex things go on. Though there is some resemblance to what happens in the real world, the game world is governed by its own special rules. A game of chess is another universe where another special set of rules determines what happens.

The rules governing the way things happen in the one proper world that we know are so familiar that it is easy to suppose that the same rules must apply everywhere else. If you drop a bottle it falls to the ground. But there are other universes where it would behave differently. In one of these other universes the bottle would remain floating where it was released. In another one the bottle might actually go upwards. The bottle would in each case be behaving according to the rules of the universe in which it was placed. In the universe of a spaceship the bottle would remain where it had been released. In an underwater universe the bottle would float upwards if it were empty or sink if it were full.

When one puts a plate on a table one expects it to stay there until one takes it off again or something else happens. If the room is locked up, one may come back years later and still find the plate where it had been left. One takes this for granted because one knows the rules. But it is possible to imagine very different universes with very different rules. A highly artificial universe might consist of a greenhouse inside which everything was made of ice. In such a universe the permanence of objects that we take for granted would no longer hold. A plate placed on the table would immediately start fading away – so would the table.

The universe we know has three dimensions, and again we take this for granted. What would happen in a universe with only two dimensions? Everything would be flat, and very different, but what went on in such a universe would be consistent with the rules of a two-dimensional universe. An ordinary photograph is a conversion of a three-dimensional universe into a two-dimensional one. So is a television screen. Neither are true two-dimensional universes because one still makes allowance for the third dimension. If someone enters a house on the television screen we do not suppose him to be merging with the house itself, as would be inevitable in a two-dimensional universe. With two dimensions there can be no 'in front of' or 'behind' or 'within'.

The difficult thing is to realize that different universes have different rules of their own. One has to try and find out what those rules are in order to understand how things happen in that universe. It is not very useful to try and describe the goings-on as if they were happening according to the rules of the universe with which we are most familiar. The awkward point is to decide when the rules of behaviour in a situation are sufficiently consistent to make up a universe of their own. The rules are determined by the organization of the system; the actual material of the system may still obey the rules of another universe. Thus people are basically the same people, but the rules may be very different in different social universes.

When one tries to apply the rules of one universe to explain the behaviour in another, a great deal of difficulty can arise. This can result in very cumbersome explanations, or ones that just do not make sense. This would happen to someone who tried to play Monopoly not according to the rules of the game but according to the rules governing real-life commerce.

The other difficulty arises when one tries to translate what is happening in a new universe into a form that makes sense in the old universe. If you try and represent a three-dimensional globe on a two-dimensional map there is that familiar distortion that makes Greenland and Siberia look so enormous. This sort of distortion is inescapable, for if something is consistent with the rules of one universe it cannot be just as consistent with the different rules of another universe.

One needs to recognize the existence of special universes and learn their special rules of behaviour; then one can understand what goes on in those universes in terms of their own rules. The rules of the universe are determined by the organization of that universe, and one must look at this in order to learn the rules.

In a previous section it was pointed out that what a memory-surface did to the material it received depended on the rules of that surface. In turn, the rules depend on the organization of that surface. In fact the surface constitutes a universe in which things can only happen in a certain way. What happens in such a universe need not parallel what happens in the physical universe, or even in the universe we know. Nor need the processes be the processes which we take for granted as the only possible ones because we have grown up with them. It is possible to have a universe in which one plus one equals one and not two.

CHAPTER 7

POLYTHENE AND PINS MODEL

As we have seen, there are some memory-surfaces which do not just passively record what is put onto them but actually alter the material. A simple and rather interesting model of such a memory-surface can be made with polythene and pins.

A number of pins are stuck just far enough into a white board for them to stand firmly upright. On the heads of the pins is laid a thin polythene sheet which covers the whole board. This is the memory-surface. The input to this memory-surface consists of drops of coloured water which are sprayed from above onto the polythene sheet. These are just as much an input as the rays of light which fall on a film to give the memory-trace known as a photograph. The memory-trace on the polythene sheet is the pattern made by the coloured water wherever this settles.

For the first experiment the coloured water is sprayed quite randomly over the whole surface without any attempt to produce a pattern. But even though the spraying is quite haphazard, at the end of it definite pools of coloured water

Fig. 12

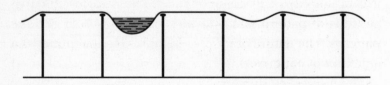

Fig. 13

will be found to form a pattern against the white board; something like the patterns shown on page 66. It appears that the memory-surface has been so active that it has in fact *created* a pattern out of a random input.

It is unlikely, however, that the input could ever have been truly random, no matter how hard one might have tried to make it so. The water may have been sprayed a little more heavily in some areas than in others; some areas may have been sprayed earlier than other areas; the polythene may not have been exactly level to start with; the pins may not have been evenly spaced. All these are very small differences; but just enough for the water to collect in one spot rather than in another. The weight of the water would then depress the polythene sheet in that spot. As the polythene sheet is depressed, the water runs off the surrounding areas into that depression, so making the depression deeper. The deeper the depression the more water it collects. And so the process goes on until at the end there is a definite pattern of pools of water instead of an even layer of water over the whole surface.

Even though this rather special type of memory-surface does not actually create patterns out of nothing, it does greatly amplify small differences. It takes hesitant little suggestions of pattern and builds them up into bold definite patterns. The nature of the system makes it an amplifier and a definer of patterns.

The interesting thing is that the memory-surface does not actually do anything. It is quite passive. In the case of the corrugated surface onto which marbles were dropped it was the surface which moved the marbles about and so processed the pattern. But with the polythene and pins model it is the water and not the polythene which organizes the pattern. The system is a self-organizing and a self-maximizing one. The polythene and pins arrangement merely allows the input to organize itself. The memory-surface carries out no active processing, it passively provides an opportunity for the information to be self-organizing. This difference between active processing and merely allowing information to process itself is a very fundamental one and a very important one.

In the second experiment the water is not sprayed randomly but made to fall in a definite pattern. This can be done by puncturing the bottom of a large can with a certain pattern of holes, through which the water drips onto the polythene surface. The pattern that forms on the surface resembles the pattern of holes in the bottom of the can. There may be some distortion, for a pool of water cannot form on top of a pin but only between the pins, but on the whole the pattern will be recorded as it has been received.

If the same pattern is put onto a polythene surface which already holds another pattern that has been put on it before, then the result may be different. When the new pattern does not overlap the established one then the new pattern is accepted as if it were on a virgin surface. But if the new pattern does fall across part of the established pattern then the incoming pattern is likely to be much altered. The pattern already on the surface will have changed the smooth surface into a contoured one. There will be valleys and pools where the water lies, and ridges and hills where the water can no longer settle. Where the incoming pattern falls onto these contours it has to follow them, even if this means a shift from the position it ought to occupy. The water will run off the ridges and into the valleys. Thus if one were to try and impose a straight line pattern athwart a similar pattern that was already established on the surface, then the new pattern would not be recorded but the old one would be reinforced (see below).

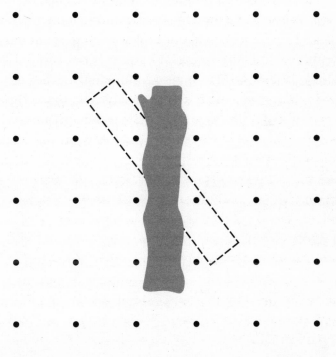

Fig. 14

This behaviour of the memory-surface shows how old patterns come to interact with new ones. It shows that the old patterns can actually determine how the new ones are received. This can mean that new information may only be received in terms of the old patterns.

The way a new pattern which is close to an old pattern flows into this and reinforces it can be very useful from a practical point of view. It means that a pattern does not have to be repeated in exactly the same way for it to become well established. If the different patterns, or presentations of the same pattern, are similar enough, then the special properties of the surface will lead to their being treated as identical. This leads to the development of definite patterns even if the input shows much variation. Here again the behaviour of the surface is directed to defining and establishing patterns. It is not the surface itself which is processing the incoming pattern but the previous patterns which have themselves altered the surface. It is the memory of previous patterns that processes the new one.

An obvious advantage of this type of system is that things go on building up with a useful continuity. The disadvantage of the system is that it becomes very difficult to change the old patterns. The established patterns are like the streams and rivers that are formed on the surface of the land by the action of rain. Once the streams and rivers have become established they tend to become self-perpetuating as they drain off into themselves whatever rain falls on the land.

SUMMARY

The polythene and pins memory-surface does not process incoming information but offers an opportunity for the information to process itself. The general effect is to define, amplify, build up and establish fixed patterns out of information which may be rather confused. This effect is achieved by allowing incoming information to organize itself, and by allowing already established patterns to guide this organization. Above all, the system is a self-organizing and a self-maximizing one.

This type of surface could be called a preferability surface. Water sprayed randomly on an ordinary type of surface would wet it evenly all over. But on a preferability surface a few deep holes would develop and water would collect in these. In effect, certain areas of the surface come to be preferred by the incoming information.

CHAPTER 8

THOUSAND BULB MODEL

The polythene and pins memory-surface processed the information that was put onto it. All this processing involved was that the water did not stay where it fell but flowed over the contours of the surface to find its own level. Apart from flowing, it also altered the contours of that surface. This shift in the position of the water means a shift in the memory pattern; a shift in the memory pattern means a change in the memory pattern; a change in the memory pattern means a processing of the information. It is as if one tried to take a photograph of a camel, but each time the pattern on the photographic plate shifted to give a picture of the pyramids. The plate would be processing the camel pattern to change it into the pyramids pattern.

The fundamental activity involved is flow. Flow means that the water moves from one area to another area. Water tends to flow downhill. This is not so easy to describe in functional terms, apart from saying that one area is preferable to another. There is a natural direction of flow, and this is determined by the contours of the surface which make some areas preferable to others.

One can now try and translate this flow principle and the general behaviour of the polythene and pins memory-surface to a new model.

There are advertising displays that consist of a surface which is made up of hundreds of separate bulbs. Different pictures can be shown on this surface by lighting up different patterns of bulbs. Pictures can also be made to flow across the surface by lighting up new bulbs and turning off lighted ones.

The new model memory-surface is made up in a similar manner. Instead of the surface being a homogenous sheet like the polythene sheet it is made up from a huge number of separate points, and each point is a bulb. Each bulb can either be on or off. As with the advertising display, the pattern on the memory-surface is given by the arrangement of lighted bulbs.

A bright pattern falling on this memory-surface would light up those bulbs on which the pattern fell. If a square pattern were put onto the surface then a square pattern of bulbs would light up. This would be arranged by having each bulb operated by a very special switch.

There are street lights which automatically turn on at dusk because the level of daylight has fallen below a certain level. The special switches in the model would work the other way round. When the light falling on the switch exceeded a certain level then the bulb would go on. This would apply to light from any source except the bulb itself (the switch would be shielded from this).

The distribution of light in this model would be equivalent to the distribution of water in the polythene and pins model. But what about the all-important flow behaviour?

To understand this, one has to go back to the tilting board on which were placed the columns of children's blocks. As the board was tilted, the taller columns toppled over. The ones that toppled over were made taller still and that made them still easier to topple over. The degree of tilt required to topple a column over could be called the toppling point. Nothing would happen until the degree of tilt reached the toppling point, but when it had then the column would take off on its own and fall over. The interesting point here is that the column would not just gradually lean over until it was lying flat but that at a certain point it would take off on its own and suddenly topple right over. In other words it needed prodding up to a point but then it would go over on its own. This toppling point could be called a threshold for action. Below this threshold nothing would happen. Once it was reached things would take off on their own.

As the columns got taller and taller the toppling point would be reached sooner and sooner. The threshold for action would be reached sooner and sooner. The threshold could be said to get lower and lower.

We can now go back to the bulbs with their special switches. These switches would behave like the block-columns. Once their threshold was reached they would switch on by themselves. Each time they switched on, the threshold for switching would get lower (just as the columns became easier to topple each time they were toppled).

This difference in ease of switching depending on what had happened in the past would be equivalent to the contours in the polythene and pins model. Those switches which were hard to activate (high thresholds) would correspond to the peaks on the polythene sheet, while those which were easy to activate (low thresholds) would correspond to the valleys.

Whenever there was a pattern of light on the memory-surface there would be an edge to it. At this edge there would be lighted bulbs next to bulbs which were unlit. The light-sensitive switches on the unlit bulbs would respond to the already lit bulbs and would tend to light up their own bulbs. Thus the pattern would tend to spread at the edges just as the water tended to flow in the polythene and pins model. Those switches with low thresholds would light up more easily than those with high thresholds, and so the pattern would tend to spread towards areas which had been activated before, just as the water in the other model tended to flow downhill towards areas which had been used before.

Whether an individual light bulb was lighted or not would depend on two things. First, whether the pattern actually fell across it. Second, whether the pattern spread to it. And the ease with which the pattern spread would depend on how often that particular bulb had been lighted previously.

At first sight such a model would seem to give a fairly good imitation of the polythene and pins surface. The reason for having this additional model is that its behaviour is much more like the organization of the nerves in the brain. The nerve network consists of a collection of individual switches which may be either on or off. Each switch has a threshold for activation and once this is reached the switch flips over by itself.

Unfortunately there is one huge difference between the polythene and pins model and the light bulb model. In the polythene and pins model there is a limited quantity of water. This water cannot be in two places at once. So if the water flows towards one area it must flow away from another area. This gives genuine pattern-shifting from one area to another according to the contours of the surface. This genuine shift of pattern gives true information-processing. Things are different in the light bulb model.

In the light bulb model the edges of the pattern will spread. New bulbs will light up and the pattern will be extended. The vital difference, however, is that though new bulbs light up, the bulbs already alight remain lighted. Thus there is no genuine shift of pattern from one area to another. The pattern just gets bigger and more blurred around the edges, but does not actually shift. It is true that the extension of the pattern will be towards the light bulbs with low thresholds, but this does not improve things if the already-lit bulbs with high thresholds remain lighted. It is as if in the polythene model the water filled the valleys but remained on the peaks as well.

As things stand, what one would get from a simple pattern put onto the light bulb surface would be a much enlarged and blurred pattern. Perhaps the whole surface would light up eventually. Unless there is genuine shift, and not just spread, then there is no useful information-processing but just a mess.

The difference between the two models is that in the polythene model it is the water itself which moves across the surface, and there is a limited amount of water. In the light bulb model the input just triggers off the light switching and there is no limit to this.

If the number of lights that were lit at any one moment

were strictly limited, then the light bulb model would better resemble the polythene one and would be a useful system. In fact this can be arranged quite neatly by making use of a circular systems effect.

CHAPTER 9

CIRCULAR SYSTEMS

On a cold winter morning a weak battery is unable to start the car engine at once. Continued use of the starter weakens the battery even further.

The autumn leaves blowing along a street pile up behind some small obstacle and so make it larger. More leaves pile up behind the larger obstacle and make it larger still. The same thing happens in winter with driven snow.

Rich people get richer. Once they have started to get rich then they have more money to play around with, their credit is better and their reputation encourages other people to lend them more capital to work with.

Big newspapers get bigger. The bigger the circulation the more advertising they attract. The more advertising they carry the more pages and better features they can afford. The more interesting the paper the bigger the circulation gets.

When people buy stocks and shares in times of inflation the stock-exchange prices rise; so more people want to buy stocks and shares in order to benefit from the price rise; so the price continues to rise.

These are all examples of one type of circular system. This is the explosive type of system which is also known as the positive feedback type. One effect leads through a series of other effects back to itself. So any change is fed back to increase that change. This type of circular system is the 'change' type. The examples used so far are all of change in an upward direction, but exactly the same system can increase change in the downward direction.

Outside the welfare state a sick person will get sicker. Being sick he earns less money. Having less money he cannot afford proper food or medical attention, so he gets sicker and that lowers his earning capacity even further.

A small newspaper tends to get smaller. As its circulation falls, so the advertising falls off. So the pages get fewer and they buy less costly features. So the circulation falls further still. When the prices fall on the stock market people tend to sell, and this drives the prices lower so more people sell. There are safeguards to prevent it happening again, but this sort of process was responsible for the great Wall Street crash. Confidence grows by feeding on itself in a circular fashion, but it also diminishes in the same way.

As soon as a few strands start to break in a rope that is supporting weight, then the strain on the remaining strands increases and some of these give way. This puts even more strain on the other strands. And so it goes on until the rope gives way completely.

Several examples of this type of system are to be found in the models already described in this book. In the case of the tilting board with the toppling columns there is an obvious positive feedback: a taller column is more likely to topple over; the more it topples over the taller it is made.

In the polythene and pins model, when the weight of water depresses an area of polythene then more water runs into that area, so the area gets even more depressed. Taken as a whole, what happens on the polythene memory-surface is that the patterns shape contours, which then organize incoming patterns, which themselves affect the contours.

If the first type of circular system is the 'change' system then the other type is the 'no change' system. This is the stabilizing type of system as opposed to the explosive nature of the first type. Here an effect leads through a series of other effects back to itself in the same circular fashion as before. But this time the effect has been reversed by the time it comes back. So a tendency to increase comes back as a tendency to decrease; this counteracts the change and keeps the system stable. This type of system is also known as the negative feedback type.

Bicycles do not ride themselves. They require someone to ride them and convert a tendency to fall over into an action that will counteract this tendency – like a movement of the handlebars. Aeroplanes do not fly themselves. They also require someone at the controls to counteract any tendency to veer off an even keel. The pilot acts as that link in the circular system that reverses the direction of something that is happening and feeds it back to prevent it happening.

If awful Johnny is being naughty in a neighbour's garden and is picking the heads off the tulips, his mother shouts at him. Johnny stops, one hopes, and the tulip system is stabilized. The decapitated tulips have acted via Johnny's mother to prevent further decapitation.

Water rising in the lavatory cistern lifts the ballcock and turns the water off. Thus the rise in water level is used to prevent a further rise in water level.

These are the two basic types of circular system, and their operation is straightforward. It is when these basic systems are combined that interesting things start to happen. Most of the behaviour of the special memory-surface described in this book depends on circular system effects.

NOTATION

In dealing with systems of this sort it is useful to have some sort of visual notation so that one can follow what happens without having to imagine the circular effects in one's head. A very simple notation is shown on page 82.

Any one thing which tends to make a second thing go in the same direction as itself is connected to the second thing by a line, which is interrupted by a solid circle. The direction of effect is shown by an arrow. If the effect can also act in the reverse direction, then there has to be a separate line and a separate arrow. If the first thing tends to get bigger, then the second thing will also tend to get bigger. If the first thing tends to get smaller, then the second thing will also tend to get smaller.

When the first thing has an opposite effect on the second thing then the connecting line is interrupted by an open circle. Thus when the first thing gets bigger the second thing gets smaller.

When the first thing gets smaller the second thing gets bigger.

In other words the filled circle indicates an exciting increase effect, and the open circle an inhibiting decrease effect.

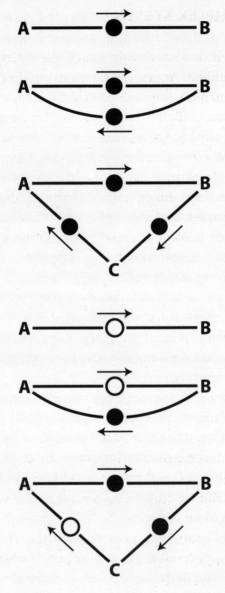

Fig. 15

MORE COMPLEX SYSTEMS

Suppose there was an area in which there were plenty of good jobs unfilled. At first people from another area might be reluctant to move into the opportunity area, as they would feel lonely without their friends and neighbours. A few people would move anyway. Once a few people had moved then it would be easier for others to move as well. Once others had moved it would become even easier for still others to move in. This increasing influx of workers would gradually saturate the labour market, and the work prospects which had been so good would become less and less good. Finally the work opportunities would decline to such an extent that people would actually start to move out of the area. The number of those moving in would also decrease.

In this situation there are two circular systems working alongside each other. In the first system, the more people who move to the opportunity area, the more attractive it becomes for their friends. In the second system, the more people who move to the area, the worse the work opportunities become and the less attractive the area becomes. One system is of the positive feedback type and the other is of the negative feedback type. Since work is the dominant factor the stabilizing system will prevail, and the situation will settle down with a limited number of people in the area. That is the basic behaviour of the system (see (a) page 85). The most fascinating thing about this system is that it is a selective one. As the work opportunities get less the people who are already there but are not desperate for jobs and can find these anywhere will tend to leave. Meanwhile only the most desperate will continue to move into the area. The number of people in the area will remain stable as some move out and some move in. But the character of the people will change, for the easy-going ones move out and the desperate ones move in. Thus the area will come to be filled with those who are desperate for work because they cannot find it anywhere else. The system, as it were, selects out these people. One could also describe the system in terms of skilled and unskilled workers, with the unskilled ones being forced out as the skilled ones moved in.

Another example of the same type of system can be seen in a party given by undergraduates in Cambridge on the bank of the river towards the end of the summer term. Towards the end of the party a group of people stand watching on the bank as some undergraduates get into a punt. Those in the punt call to their friends on the bank to join them. At first the friends are quite happy to do so. But as more and more people get into the punt it gets lower and lower in the water until it seems very likely to sink. At this point some of the more sober and timid people start to leave the punt while their more drunk and carefree fellows are still clambering aboard. In the end the punt is filled only by the jollier under-graduates (see (b) page 85).

Again the system is a selecting one. On one hand there is the positive inducement of getting onto the punt to join one's friends, but on the other hand there is the negative inducement that the punt is about to sink. The relative strengths of the positive and negative inducements vary with the state of sobriety of each undergraduate. This means that the more inhibited undergraduates get pushed out and the more excitable ones are left. This is the type of system that provides the special memory-surface with selective capacity.

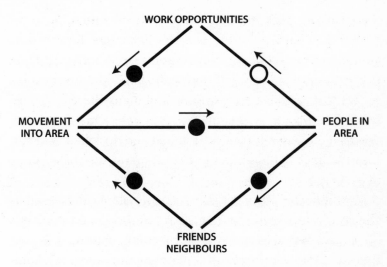

Fig. 16a

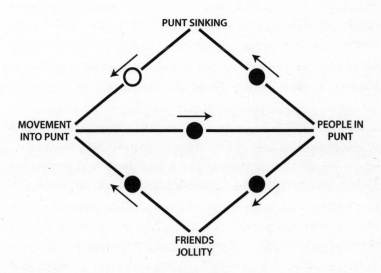

Fig. 16b

ARTIFICIAL MODELS

The behaviour of the systems described above can be imitated with a simple mechanical model. This model is shown on page 87. It consists of a flap which is attached to the wall by a hinge in such a way that the flap can fold downwards. The flap is, however, supported by a light spring which keeps it level. Small lead blocks are now put onto the platform one by one. As more blocks are added, the platform tilts more and more until some of the blocks start to slide off. Eventually only the blocks with the stickiest bottoms will be left on the platform. In this system, the more blocks there are on the platform, the more difficult it becomes for any block to stay on the platform. The presence of blocks on the platform inhibits the presence of blocks on the platform. But there is an artificial rule which states that the presence of blocks on the platform encourages the presence of other blocks on the platform: that is why they are placed there.

The system is again a self-selecting one. It would not be the same to place the blocks on a sloping surface in order to see which slid down and which did not. This would be selection by an outside agency which adjusted the slope of the surface. The lead blocks which do remain on the platform are the ones with the stickiest bottoms, just as the group in the punt was made up of the drunker undergraduates, and the group in the work area was made up of the most work-hungry people.

All three examples of the system show two effects:

1. A limited number of units in the designated area.
2. Selection of these units according to some quality which they possess to a greater extent than the others.

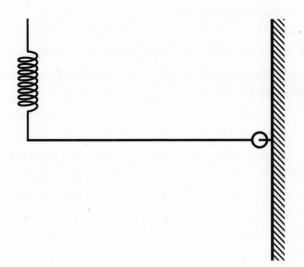

Fig. 17

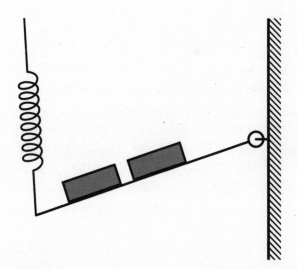

Fig. 18

The discriminating process can be quite fine. If a block that is added to the platform is only slightly more sticky than one of those already there, the platform will tilt just enough for the other one to slide off no matter how small the difference may be.

CHAPTER 10

If you pour water onto a rigid surface it will spread out over that surface. The more water you pour the bigger the pool gets. But if instead of being rigid the surface consists of a thin rubber sheet which is supported only at the edges, then a curious thing happens. The pool of water does not go on spreading but reaches a limited size. No matter how much more water is poured onto the sheet the pool does not increase in diameter. This effect is shown on page 90. What happens is that the weight of the water depresses the sheet. More water only depresses the sheet further. As the centre of the sheet is depressed, the walls of the depression get steeper and steeper and so prevent the water from spreading. In effect one has a stabilized system with the thin rubber sheet. The difficulty of spread (steepness of walls) is proportional to the amount of water, so no matter how much more water one puts onto the sheet it cannot spread. This is in sharp contrast to the unstabilized system, in which a greater amount of water means greater spread.

The trouble with the thousand bulb memory-surface was that if one allowed the pattern to spread at all, then it would spread all over the surface in a mess. What one required was

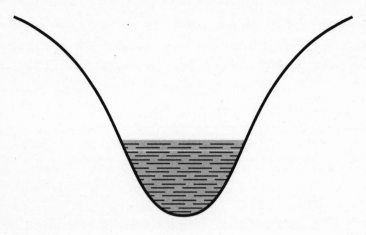

Fig. 19

that there should be only a limited number of bulbs alight, and that if new bulbs lit up, old ones would go out. This would give a genuine shift of pattern and useful information-processing. This is, after all, what happens in the advertising displays where pictures flow across the array of bulbs because new ones light up as old ones go out.

Both examples of circular system given in the previous section resulted in a limited number of units in some given area. This was achieved by combining an exciting factor with an inhibiting one. The exciting factor was job opportunity in one case and jollity in the other. The inhibiting factor was saturation of the labour market in one case and fear of a ducking in the other case. One can apply the same principles to the thousand bulb model. As in the case of the rubber sheet, the party punt and the opportunity area, one combines an exciting factor with an inhibiting factor (as shown on page 85). The exciting factor is simply the tendency of the pattern to spread, the tendency of a bulb to light up if an

adjoining bulb is already alight. The inhibiting factor has to
be built in deliberately. This factor has to be proportional to
the number of lighted bulbs and must act to make it harder
for a bulb to light up or stay alight.

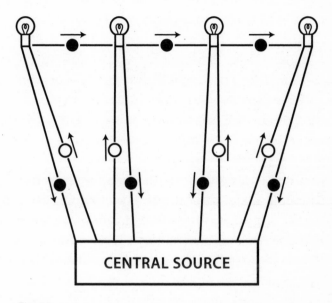

Fig. 20

It would be easy to suggest that from each bulb there was
a wire going to a central source, and that whenever a bulb
was alight then it would contribute something to this central
source. From this central source a different wire would run
back to each bulb and would make it difficult for that bulb
to light. Such an arrangement would work (as shown above)
very well. The actual layout of the connections could be organized in many different ways to give the same effect. All one

needs is an inhibiting network that is energized in proportion to the state of excitation on the surface and which tends to reduce that excitation.

The above method is, however, a very cumbersome way of achieving the effect and it is only mentioned because something of the sort goes on in the brain. For the purpose of the thousand bulb model there is a more elegant way of achieving the same effect. The model is encased in a shallow glass case. As more bulbs light up, the temperature in the glass case goes up too. Those special switches for each bulb are now made temperature sensitive so that the higher the temperature, the higher becomes the threshold of each switch, the more difficult it is to light it. This additional mechanism provides the inhibiting influence.

A small pattern falls on the thousand bulb surface. The bulbs light up under the pattern. The adjoining bulbs light up and the pattern tends to spread. But as it spreads, the temperature rises and this makes it harder and harder for the pattern to spread, as the threshold of the switches rises too. There comes a point when the temperature is such that at the edge of the pattern the threshold of the switch is so high that the light from an adjoining bulb is no longer sufficient. The pattern stops spreading.

Where the threshold of a particular switch is low, then the pattern may go on spreading in that direction, because even with the temperature effect the threshold has not yet risen to an impossible level. As the pattern spreads into these easy areas, some of the bulbs already alight may actually drop out as their switches are affected by the temperature. There is now a selecting effect operating, as there was with the punt system and the opportunity area. The more excitable units are still moving into the area (i.e. lighting up) while the less excitable units are dropping out. With this arrangement there is a limited number of bulbs alight, and this limited number is made up from the most easily lit bulbs. The pattern is now behaving as the water did in the polythene model. It is shifting bodily from one area to another.

One might think of an interesting lecture in a small room. As more people crowd into the room the temperature rises. The less interested start to leave as it becomes stuffy. But the more interested still come in. Finally the room is filled only with the more interested, more excitable people.

Whereas previously the thousand bulb model was inferior to the polythene one, it is now superior. With the polythene surface model it was difficult to see why water dripped onto an already contoured surface should ever retain the pattern in which it was dripped. Would it not always run off according to the contours? You would never be able to find out about camels if your photograph always showed the pyramids when you took a shot of a camel. In the polythene model the contours already present on the surface almost totally dominate the process and the actual incoming pattern may never survive. In the thousand bulb model there is a balance between the two.

Any individual light bulb may be on or it may be off. This depends on whether its switch is activated or not. And this in turn depends on the following factors, some of which would tend to activate it and others to keep it inactivate.

Activating factors:

1. If the pattern falls directly onto the switch (it is assumed that the patterns are presented as patterns of illumination).

2. If an adjoining bulb is alight.
3. If the threshold of the switch is low, due to frequent activation in the past. The more often it has been activated the lower will be the threshold.

Inactivating factors:

1. If none of the above factors are operating.
2. If the threshold has been raised by the temperature change due to the number of bulbs already alight.

By and large a pattern put onto the thousand bulb surface will retain its position. But if it overlaps areas where the switch threshold is unusually low due to repeated activation, then the pattern will shift to include those bulbs at the expense of ones on which the pattern actually falls. This results in a change in the pattern, in information-processing.

BEHAVIOUR OF THE THOUSAND BULB MEMORY-SURFACE

The first point is that only a limited number of bulbs can be alight at any one time on the surface. But the pattern put onto the surface may be smaller than this number or it may be larger than this number.

If the presented pattern is below this number, then that pattern will spread until the allowed number of lighted bulbs is achieved. The spread will take place in the direction of those areas which had held patterns in the past, since the thresholds will be lower in these areas. In this way a pattern comes to be extended or enlarged by the surface. The surface does not just accept the pattern but actually elaborates it in terms of what it has been connected to in the past or in terms of what it resembles.

If the pattern put onto the surface covers many more bulbs than the allowed number, then only some of the covered bulbs will light up and the others will remain inactive. The ones that light up will be those with the lowest thresholds. As far as the memory-surface is concerned the rest of the pattern is ignored (at least for the time being). The memory-surface just selects out whichever part of the pattern is most familiar and reacts to this. This is the selecting property of a memory-surface. In terms of information-processing this is certainly the most useful property of the surface. It is curious that it should arise from a defect in the surface. The defect is that the surface is unable to take in a large pattern. Yet this defect is the result of that organization of the surface which is so essential for other reasons.

What happens if two separate patterns are put onto the memory-surface? By separate patterns are meant patterns that do not overlap and are not adjacent to each other. It is extremely unlikely that two such patterns would be exactly equal in area or time of arrival. Even if they were, it is extremely unlikely that the parts of memory-surface on which they fell would be exactly equal in terms of switch thresholds and what had happened to the area just before.

The situation is equivalent to a model made of two containers connected together at the bottom by a tube as shown on page 96. Both containers are half filled with water and both are suspended by elastic bands. The container which starts with slightly more water sinks slightly lower than the other one. This causes water to flow into it from the other container,

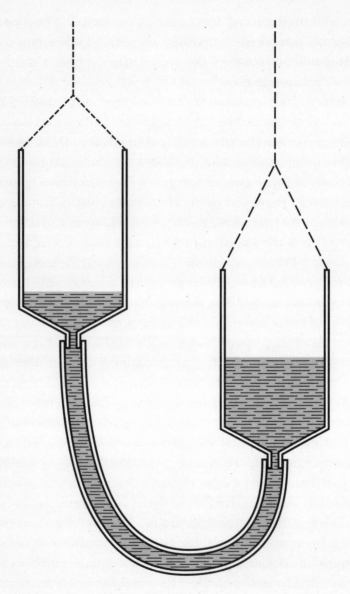

Fig. 21

and this makes it sink lower still. In the end, one container comes to hold all the water while the other one is empty. No matter how one starts off, the result will always be the same.

In the thousand bulb model exactly the same effect is obtained if the tendency of an illuminated area to enlarge is proportional to the size of that area. This may seem an arbitrary property to ascribe to the surface, but in fact it would follow quite naturally in a random network such as seems to exist in the brain. In such a network the tendency of an activated area to spread is proportional to the size of the area.

The picture on page 98 shows a simple network in which the switches are represented by dark circles. If the tendency of a switch to become activated is proportional to the number of connections between it and already active switches, then the switches marked 1, 2, 3 are more likely to be activated if all the switches inside the big circle are active than if only the ones inside the square happen to be. The bigger the activated area the more likely it is to include random connections to switches outside it.

When this property is transferred to the thousand bulb surface it makes it impossible for two separate areas of activation to coexist on the surface. The larger area will tend to get larger and this means that the smaller area will have to get smaller, since the total active area is limited. The process is another circular effect, for as the small area gets smaller its tendency to spread also gets smaller and so it continues until the area disappears. This behaviour of the memory-surface is important, because it means that there can be only one coherent area of illumination on the surface at a time. This has wide implications for the information-processing behaviour of the surface.

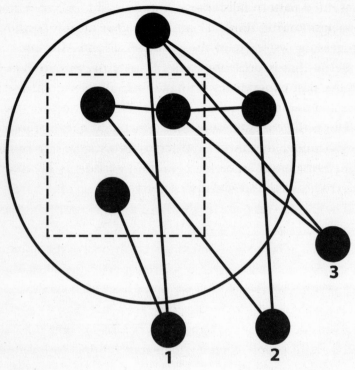

Fig. 22

SUMMARY

In the thousand bulb memory-surface, there is a single, coherent and limited area of illumination which moves about the surface according to what has happened in the past and what is happening at the moment. The area of illumination is made up from the most easily excited units on the surface. Ease of excitation of a unit is determined by how often the unit has been excited in the past, by whether the presented pattern falls across it, and by what is happening to neighbouring units. The end result is an information-processing system capable of selecting and altering the material that is presented to it. Both processes are based on the past experience of the surface. Both processes are directed towards extracting and establishing firm patterns.

This is the basic memory-surface. There are many further modifications that increase its capacity to process information. For convenience, this memory-surface is hereafter referred to as the special memory-surface.

CHAPTER 11

ATTENTION

What would you think if every time you looked in a certain mirror it showed only your mouth and ignored the rest of your face? No matter from what angle you looked, or from what distance, the mirror would still only show your mouth. Even if you got your friends to look into this peculiar mirror it would only show their mouths.

What would you think if you switched on the television set one night and instead of the whole screen lighting up there appeared a tiny circle of light which always contained the mouth of an actor or an announcer?

What would you think if you were to take a photograph of a room, and when you developed the film the only thing that appeared was a large cake on the table? You would take another photograph, from a different angle, but once again only the cake would show up. Using the same camera you would take a photograph of the high street with its various shops and stores. To your surprise the only thing that showed up on the developed film would be the cake shop.

This odd behaviour of the mirror, of the television set and

of the camera is how the special memory-surface behaves all the time. When a large pattern is put onto the surface, only a small part of the pattern is retained. The rest is simply ignored. The area of activation on the memory-surface is strictly limited and cannot exceed this size. This limited area settles on the most easily activated part of the surface, and this just means the part that has been used most frequently. That is why the mirror, the television set and the camera all limited their attention to the mouth or food.

In fact this behaviour of the memory-surface means that it is only paying attention to one part of the total available pattern. Attention is no more than dealing with one part of the environment at a time. There need be no magic about it. There need be no question of actively directing attention. The effect follows from the ordinary behaviour of a particular type of memory-surface. And the behaviour is purely passive.

It might seem that this behaviour of the special memory-surface is a shortcoming and that an effective memory-surface ought not to have such a limited outlook. In actual fact, far from being a disadvantage this limited attention span effect is so tremendous an advantage that the whole functioning of the mind depends on it. A limited attention span means that much is left out, but it also means that something is actually selected. It is this selection process, this ability to select, that is so important. Selection means preference and choice instead of total acceptance of all that is offered. It is this selection which is so often assumed to be impossible in a passive system.

How many people who drive through that area every day know that on top of every traffic light in Marylebone is a metal tongue of flame, of the variety used in depictions of souls in purgatory? For years I had been driving through the area, and presumably looking closely at the traffic lights on many occasions, but I never noticed this tongue of flame. Yet it is so close to the topmost light that from across the street the difference in visual angle must be minute. But attention settles on the traffic lights as being the important thing so everything else is ignored. Life would be difficult without this sort of selection according to usefulness.

A bathroom includes a bath, a mirror, a basin and sometimes a lavatory bowl. If one had to react to the bathroom as a whole, then it would be impossible to ever use it except to choose the wallpaper. Fortunately, attention finds itself directed to the bath, the basin or whatever else is needed.

Suppose that someone was pouring hot water from a kettle onto a slab of ordinary table jelly. Suppose that for some reason, such as the interposition of a screen, you were never able to see the whole situation but only part at a time.

If your attention is on the jelly, and nothing else, then what you see is the jelly *disappearing*.

If your attention is on the hot water as well as the jelly, what you see is the hot water *destroying* the jelly.

If your attention is on the coloured sticky fluid that is spreading over the table, then that fluid is being *created*.

If your attention is on both the jelly and the coloured fluid, then the jelly is being *converted* into the fluid.

If your attention is on the water pouring from the kettle and also on the coloured fluid (but the actual jelly is hidden behind a screen), then the water is being *altered* into coloured water.

Thus, from exactly the same situation one can obtain the concepts of disappearance, destruction, creation, conversion and alteration, depending on what attention picks out. The way a situation is looked at depends on this. The same situation may appear completely different to two different people because the contours of their memory-surfaces are such that the selected attention area or sequence of attention areas is quite different.

There is a disadvantage in this system. When a situation has two alternative explanations, both of which are equally valid, then the definitive selection capacity of the memory-surface will choose one and completely ignore the other. Sometimes the second choice may be acknowledged after the first has been dealt with, but more often the first choice sets off a train of development and the second choice is never considered at all. The two approaches to the situation may be very close to each other in terms of mathematical probability (for instance if 51 per cent of people would choose one and 49 per cent the other). Nevertheless, the nature of the memory-surface is such that it chooses one and ignores the other as completely as if the distance between the two approaches had been huge. This definitive type of selection of the memory-surface makes for great efficiency in extracting patterns from the surroundings, but it can lead to much trouble. For instance, two people faced with exactly the same situation can come to very different conclusions. What is worse is that they will be completely unable to see the validity of the other person's point of view, since the selection is an exclusive, maximized one and not a natural probability one.

There are, however, compensations. Humour depends on exactly the same process. Thus if one had a system which excluded the possibility of arrogant righteousness, as described above it would also exclude the possibility of humour. This point will be developed in a later section.

Another compensation of this maximizing type of selection shown by the memory-surface is that it makes the starvation of Balaam's ass an impossibility. Balaam's ass was stood by philosophers between two equal bundles of hay, and it was supposed to starve to death because it would be unable to choose between the two equal attractions if it behaved passively. With the type of selection shown by the memory-surface this could never occur. The slightest difference in the bundle of hay, in the remote or immediate experience of the ass, in the refraction of its two eyes, in the way the bundles had been put down, in anything at all, would be maximized by the system into a definite selection which would choose one bundle and ignore the other. In fact Balaam's ass would have had much more difficulty if one bundle was hay and the other one carrots. Because of the organization of the memory-surface this arrangement would have caused greater indecision.

The example of the selective mirror, television set and camera might have given the impression that the memory-surface would only pay attention to one part of a picture *at a time*. Attention flits from one part to another until most or all the picture has been covered. The area of activation moves across the memory-surface, flowing from one place to another according to the changing contours of the surface, just as gravy flows in a dish that is tilted now one way and then another. The way these contours change from moment to moment, and so ensure flow of the activated area, will be discussed later.

Since the attention area covers one part of the picture after another, one could say that the whole picture has been broken down into separate attention fragments.

As you slowly turn off a tap, the stream of water is gradually reduced to a trickle, and then all of a sudden the continuous trickle breaks up into a string of tiny drops. This is because there comes a point when the stream gets narrow enough for the surface tension effect to nip it into separate drops. The process involved is exactly analogous to the behaviour of the memory-surface which separates a continuous picture into fragments.

When you are in a foreign country and do not yet know the language, it just seems to be a continuous stream of incomprehensible noise. As you get to know the language it starts to break up into recognizable sounds, then into recognizable words and phrases. Now you cannot, no matter how hard you try, go back to hearing it as a continuous sound. It will always be divided into separate words. This is the way the memory-surface deals with the incomprehensible picture that is presented to it by its surroundings. As soon as some patterns start to be recognized, they form the focus for an attention area. The continuous picture is now broken up into these attention areas which become more and more definite. This is the pattern extracting process which has been stressed as a natural property of the memory-surface.

The great advantage of breaking things down into separate fragments is that the fragments have a great mobility. They can be moved around in a way that would never be possible with the whole picture. Language works because it consists of mobile fragments that can be strung together in different ways. Mathematics, science and measurement are all based on the same fragmenting process. This, then, is another tremendous advantage of the limited attention span that is a natural feature of the special memory-surface described in this book. The disadvantage is that the fragments become fixed and rigid, and since they may no longer be the most convenient fragments (though they may have been at one time) this can block the development of new ways of looking at a situation.

Although the whole picture may eventually be covered by a sequence of attention areas, the actual sequence in which the areas are covered may make a great difference to the interpretation of the picture. Thus if one starts at the centre instead of at the bottom left-hand corner the effect may be entirely different. This point will be dealt with later.

Change and selection are the basic processes of evolution. Random mutations in the genes come about through such things as cosmic radiation. These mutations become manifest as physical changes in the animal. The process of selection by survival of the fittest then preserves the most useful changes. Patterns evolve in a similar manner on the memory-surface which is capable both of inducing change and of selection. Selection is actually at two levels. The first level is the self-selection of information so that it makes sense in itself, quite apart from the selfish needs of the organism. The second type of selection is to satisfy these selfish needs.

A sieve is an example of a selecting mechanism in that it lets through only a certain size of particle. A photographic plate that is more sensitive to some colours than to others will also show selectivity in that these colours will be emphasized. This type of selection is useful in that it extracts information from the total pattern that is fed into it. But the selection is fixed and unchangeable, since it depends on the fixed properties of the system (the composition of the photographic emulsion, the size of the holes in the sieve).

With the special memory-surface, however, the fact that selection takes place at all depends on the organization of the system. The selection itself is not fixed but depends on the past experience of the surface. Thus it is a self-selecting system in that the accumulation of past information comes to select the new information. This leads to continuity which, as we have seen, has such tremendous advantages in making sense of the environment, but also has some disadvantages.

SINGLE ATTENTION AREA

The area of activation on the special memory-surface is not only limited in size, but it must also be single and coherent. Two small and separate areas which would together add up to the permitted size will not do.

There is no difficulty in taking a photograph of two people in a room. You can even put two pictures side by side and take a photograph of the two so that both are shown on the same piece of paper. This is quite possible with the memory-surface of the film. The special memory-surface, however, would only show one person at a time.

As far as the memory-surface is concerned, separate patterns are simply patterns that have become established on their own. If two such separate patterns are presented to the memory-surface, three things can happen.

One pattern may be accepted and may then be elaborated further with the other pattern being ignored.

One pattern may be accepted first and then the second pattern may be accepted afterwards. And this may establish a sequence.

Fig. 23

Fig. 24

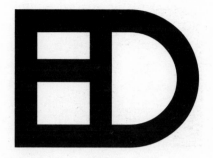

Fig. 25

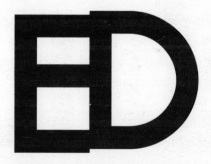

Fig. 26

The two separate patterns might, with repetition, become amalgamated to form a single pattern.

The whole tendency of the special memory-surface is to establish separate patterns and to go on reinforcing that separateness. On page 108 and 109 is shown a continuous picture which has been separated by the memory-surface into two attention areas, into two patterns. The possibility of establishing a single attention area that straddles the two is remote, since attention will follow the line of separation.

How, then, do two separate patterns come to combine into a single pattern? If the patterns occur in sequence, so that attention moves from one pattern to the other and back again, then the short-term memory properties of the surface may combine them into a single pattern. From the alternation of the two patterns may emerge a third pattern which combines them both. The two separate patterns may be combined to form a new pattern, or they may just be combined to form a sequence so that one pattern will always follow the other.

This combining property of the special memory-surface ultimately depends on the necessity for the activated area to be single and coherent.

The separating property of the special memory-surface leads to discrimination and selection. The combining property leads to association and learning.

CHAPTER 12

JELLY MODEL

What happens to patterns put onto the memory-surface is largely determined by the traces left on the surface by previous patterns. The memory-surface is no more than a system which allows past information to interact with present information in a self-organizing, self-selecting and self-maximizing fashion.

The position and movement of the activated area on the memory-surface depend on the contours, and these are largely determined by what has happened on the surface before. One needs a model in which a pattern put onto a surface will leave a permanent trace that will affect the next pattern that is put onto the surface. In this way, the contours of the surface will be a sculpted record of all that has happened to the surface.

An ordinary fruit jelly made up in a shallow dish provides just such a model. The flat surface of the jelly is the virgin memory-surface. The incoming pattern is hot water spooned onto the surface at different places. Since the area of activation is limited, only a fixed dollop of hot water is used as provided by a teaspoon. While it is still hot the water dissolves the gelatin. The water is then poured off, leaving a shallow impression in the surface. A fresh dollop is added. In this way the surface of the jelly is sculpted into contours which depend on where the hot water has been placed. Once depressions and channels have formed, then the water will no longer stay where it is placed but will flow away to a new position. For instance, if the second dollop of water flows into the depression formed by the first one, then that depression will be made deeper but there will be very little erosion where the second dollop was actually placed. In this way the incoming patterns are moved around by the contours sculpted by previous patterns, and in the process these contours are made even more definite.

The jelly model imitates the special memory-surface in the following manner:

1. Water will tend to flow towards the lower areas just as activation flows towards low threshold units.
2. Once water has flowed through an area it is more likely to do so again, just as activation lowers the threshold of a unit and makes it more likely to be activated again.
3. The area covered by the water is limited, as is the area of activation.
4. The area covered by the water is coherent, like the area of activation.

With this jelly model one can now see what happens to the natural flow of activation on a memory-surface with these characteristics. The basic function of the model is similar to the polythene and pins one, but with the jelly, memories can be accumulated and the surface properly sculpted by them. Water placed at one spot on the jelly surface may flow off along some channel and end up somewhere else. What does this flow represent? In the first place, the interpretation and recording of the incoming information. Recording is not an isolated process but may involve interpretation, which includes a string of images. In the second place, the flow of the water across different parts of the memory-surface represents the different images of a train of thought that might be set off by incoming information. The main point is that there is flow, and that the flow is dictated by the contours of the surface.

Many of the things that happen on the jelly surface illustrate the behaviour of the special memory-surface.

CENTRING

The first dollop of water leaves a shallow depression. If another dollop is placed so that it spreads into the first depression then the water will flow into that depression. If further dollops are placed all around the initial depression in a similar overlapping manner, then the initial depression will get deeper and deeper even though no further water has been placed directly in this area. This implies that patterns which are linked up to one central pattern will establish that central pattern very firmly. It also means that a pattern may be reinforced by a succession of other patterns that are similar but not exactly the same. It also means that the memory-surface can extract one fixed pattern from a succession of overlapping but different patterns.

ASSIMILATION

The water that flows into an adjacent depression instead of staying where it has been placed indicates that it is almost impossible to establish a new pattern which is closely related to an old pattern. The new pattern is assimilated by the old pattern and does not become established as a separate pattern.

FIXED PATTERNS

Once the channels and depressions have become sculpted into the surface, then it becomes difficult to alter them, since any new patterns tend to follow the old contours and to reinforce them rather than alter them.

LINKED PATTERNS

If a succession of dollops of water are placed so that each one overlaps the preceding one to form a chain, then the water always flows through this chain to end up in the original position. This implies that a chain of successive connected images will always lead back to the original image, no matter how far it is extended. This also implies that one pattern can lead directly to another which at first sight seems very remote unless one knows the sequence that connects the two.

BACKBONE CHANNEL

Quite often the jelly surface develops a deep and narrow backbone channel which connects various shallow impressions. Since the channel drains all these areas, the flow through it is much greater than through the other areas, and the channel becomes deep. This may represent a unifying theme or organizational pattern that develops to link up otherwise separate patterns. The interesting thing is that this channel becomes more firmly established than what it is linking up.

REPRESENTATIVE PART

Where the flow is through a series of linked depressions, as on page 116, a narrow channel may develop down the centre of each depression and carry all the flow. This suggests that only part of a pattern may come to represent it in a train of images. This part is symbolic, or representative, of the whole. It may also imply that only that part of the pattern which is relevant to the train of images becomes properly established.

TIME SEQUENCE

Even though a number of dollops of water are placed in exactly the same positions on the jelly surface, the actual sequence in which they are placed can make a huge difference to the resulting pattern. The pictures on page 117 show what happens when the same areas are activated in a different sequence. In each case the deepest hole (the best established pattern) is to be found in a different position. This means that the memory-surface does not accumulate memories by simple addition. Since each memory is processed by the preceding memories, the actual sequence of presentation may make a very great difference to the pattern that is established, even though the individual patterns presented may be the same.

Fig. 27

Fig. 28

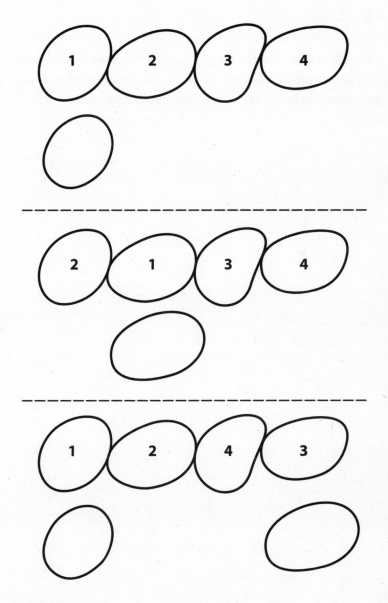

Figs. 29–31

SUMMARY

The jelly model is a very simple memory-surface. Its advantage is that it provides a system in which incoming information is processed by information that is already recorded.

CHAPTER 13

You are sitting alone in a strange, dark room. As the light gets better yon begin to see the vague outlines of shapes around you. Your imagination interprets these shapes according to the little that you can see, and largely in terms of what seems most likely from your experience. As the light increases the actual nature of the objects becomes more obvious. The pattern presented by the objects tends to take over from the pattern elaborated by the imagination.

With the jelly model, once the contours had developed, any new spoonful of water rarely stayed where it was put, for it flowed off into some channel or depression. This would mean that any incoming pattern would be seen entirely in terms of past experience as a repetition of an old pattern. Such a system would be extremely rigid and incapable of change. It would be much more useful if the incoming pattern tended to stick where it landed and also tended to flow. Whether it stuck or whether it flowed would depend on a balance between the intensity of the pattern and the slope of the contours. This is the effect that was described for the thousand bulb model. In the darkened room analogy, the intensity of the image would be low at first, and so there

Edward de Bono

would be a tendency to much flow and elaboration of what could be seen. As the light increased so would the intensity of the pattern, which would tend to stick more where it landed. This is purely an analogy to illustrate a balance between the tendency of a pattern to stick or to shift.

If the limited area of activation on the memory-surface has become stationary at one point, why should it ever shift?

In the jelly model, once the water has reached the lowest point of the surface, why should it ever shift?

If the attention area has settled on some part of a pre-sented picture, such as the mouth, why should it ever shift?

One might say that attention would shift because the actual picture placed before the surface was shifting as the pattern on a television screen might shift. One might say that even if the picture was stationary one's eyes might move over it for some mechanical reason. These explanations would only be a very partial explanation. To some extent attention is dependent on the presented pattern in the way that one's eye is caught by a bright object. But even if the external picture remains the same, attention can still wander over it. There is also the situation where there is no presented picture at all, but simply a train of images or thought which reflects shift-ing activity on the memory-surface.

With the thousand bulb model, the pattern of lights would shift until the lights with the lowest threshold were lit up. But once that position had been reached then it could only alter if some new area became relatively more easily activated, or if the lit-up area became relatively more difficult to activate. For the pattern to shift from an optimal area there has to be some sort of tiring factor, so that a unit which was alight would gradually tire. The threshold of that unit would rise as it tired, and so excitation would shift to another unit whose threshold had by comparison become lower. Such a tiring factor would cause the limited area of activation to pause in a favoured area, but then to shift to another area as the threshold of the favoured area rose. It would be like a pool of water lying on a plastic sheet. If the sheet were raised by prodding it from below whenever the water settled, the pool would shift to a new position each time.

This tiring factor is known as adaptation in the nervous system and is a well-recognized phenomenon.

SWIFT FLOW AND STACCATO FLOW

In the jelly model the flow down the channels is swift and continuous. A swift and continuous flow means that the water at each moment has ahead of it an area that is lower than the one it is on. The same swift flow can occur on the special memory-surface. If there is a row of units with decreasing thresholds, so that the threshold of each one is less than that of the preceding unit, then activation will flow swiftly along the whole row without any pauses. This would be equivalent to instant interpretation of a pattern, to intuition, inspiration or imageless thought.

The other sort of flow on the special memory-surface is jerky or staccato in nature. The activity pauses in a favoured area. As that area tires, the activity moves on to another area where it again pauses. If the memory-surface were smooth, then this would still give a relatively smooth movement. But if the surface is contoured, then the movement can become jerky. Instead of being movement down a smooth slope it becomes movement down a series of terraces, as shown in (b) on page 123. The water pauses on one terrace until the lip of that terrace is dissolved, and then goes with a rush to the next terrace where it again pauses. On the memory-surface, of course, there is not a fixed terrace slope but an area that becomes relatively elevated by the tiring factor. Nor is it the lip of the terrace that dissolves.

On page 124 (a) is shown a profile across a contour on the memory-surface. The area of activation as represented by a pool of water is resting in a favoured area, or hollow. The tiring factor which raises the threshold of units is represented by gradually raising the floor of the hollow as in pulling up a rug. In the first picture, when the floor had been raised high enough, the flow into the next area would be smooth. In the second picture, it would be with a rush.

If the shifting area of activation touches upon a low threshold area then it becomes shifted into that area with a rush. This gives a staccato type of flow with a rapid snapping from one position to another with pauses in between. This is equivalent to a succession of images that make up a thought pattern. There may be a gradual change or a rapid snapping from one to the other. The interesting point is that the images are just pauses in the flow of activation. They are indications of what is happening, they do not themselves direct anything. If a car were travelling from London to Edinburgh and the occupant stopped in every major town en route to telephone and report where he was, this would not itself affect the route he took. Thought is a flow of activation across a passive memory-surface, not an active stringing together of items from a memory store.

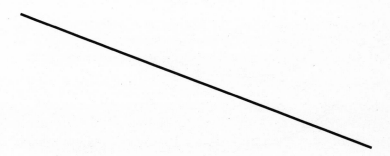

Fig. 32a

Fig. 32b

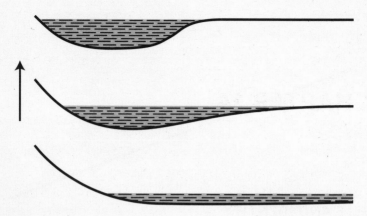

Fig. 33a

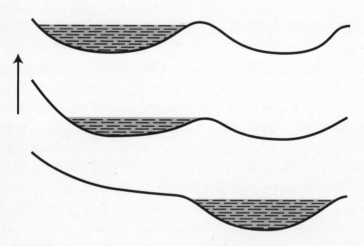

Fig. 33b

CHAPTER 14

SELF AND IDENTITY

Freddie was designed as a space-age pet for modern living. He is a small black sphere which is completely smooth on the outside. When Freddie is kicked he starts to roll about. To stop him you kick him again. Whenever he comes up against an obstacle he backs away, moves along it or round it, or just changes direction, as he feels inclined. The purpose of Freddie is to provide intelligent animation without his owner having to feed him, look after him or take him round the lamp-posts every evening.

If you are sitting in a darkened room facing a wall over which a bright disc of light is playing, you soon come to be aware only of the disc of light. As it darts about from one place to another, now hovering, now moving swiftly, now circling about some point, the disc seems to have an animation and a purpose of its own.

Anything that moves around on its own without any obvious outside agency directing the movement seems to have identity and animation. On the special memory-surface there is an area of activation which is limited, coherent and shifts around on its own. With the thousand bulb model this is actually an area of illumination, like the disc of light on the wall. As it plays around it might seem to have a self and a purpose of its own.

If you are back in that darkened room again, and instead of the playful disc of light a series of pictures start to flash on the wall, you would assume that there was someone behind you with a slide projector. Because something seems to be happening with a reason, because there appears to be a deliberate choice, one assumes that an outside agent must be making this choice.

Suppose that the wall of the room was hung with a number of different photographs and that the disc of light returned to play over these, choosing now one and now another. One might get the impression that the disc was intelligently choosing the pictures, or that someone was directing the light over the pictures. Finally, suppose that the pictures simply lit up from behind one after another in a sequence, so that only one picture was illuminated at a time. What would one assume? Would one assume that this was a self-selecting property of the pictures, or would one assume that there was someone, somewhere, operating switches?

The pictures that light up one after another are like the patterns that follow each other on the special memory-surface. It is actually the pictures themselves that in sequence attract the illumination, and not an area of illumination that seeks out the pictures. So on the self-selecting surface of the thousand bulb model the area of light shifts about, giving first one pattern and then another. Exactly the same effect can be obtained on the advertising displays where someone flicks over the switches to make certain patterns of bulbs light up one after another. The ultimate effect is the same, and because it is the same it does not indicate how it has been brought about.

If the special memory-surface can be said to have a self through having choice and movement, could it also have a self-consciousness? Perhaps all one would need to do would be to put a mirror above the surface.

CHAPTER 15

In any communication situation there is one person trying to say something and another person trying to understand what is being said. Perception could be regarded as communication between the environment and the mind. Only the environment is not trying very hard. So the mind has to try hard enough for both of them. This is the memory-surface making sense out of a confusion of patterns that are available to it.

There are three basic types of communication:

1. Communication by transfer.
2. Communication by confusion.
3. Communication by trigger.

Communication by transfer is simple enough. A pattern at one point is communicated in such a way that the very same pattern can be repeated somewhere else. The pattern is bodily transferred. A photograph is an approximation to communication by transfer in so far as the picture of the environment is transferred to a piece of paper. The North Atlantic cable that carries telephone conversations under the ocean is communication by transfer, as the hope is to repeat at the one end the exact sounds that are put in at the other end. Some teachers believe that the function of teaching is to transfer what is in the textbooks into the minds of reluctant pupils.

Communication by confusion is when you present a mess to the other person and expect him to make something out of it. You expect him to make something out of it because you are confident that he has the equipment to do so. The actual pattern he extracts will, however, depend on him as an individual, whereas with communication by transfer the pattern is the same for all who receive it. Much of modern art is communication by confusion. A bewilderment of sensations, a montage of images is flung at the viewer, and as with a flung custard pie some of it sticks in the form of individual reaction. Communication by confusion is also the initial stage of the relationship between the memory-surface and the environment. The memory-surface picks out its own individual patterns from the confusion offered to it.

Communication by trigger occurs when all that is passed over is a single trigger word which unlocks a complete pattern in the receiver. The trigger word, clue or symbol merely identifies which pattern the receiver must use. The receiver is already stocked with patterns as a library is with books. The trigger identifies the pattern as a library reference number identifies a book. There is a huge difference between communicating the contents of a book by reading it over the telephone, and just communicating the library reference number and letting the person read the book himself. Some forms of art communicate in this way, by offering a minimal but pregnant stimulus which draws forth elaborate patterns

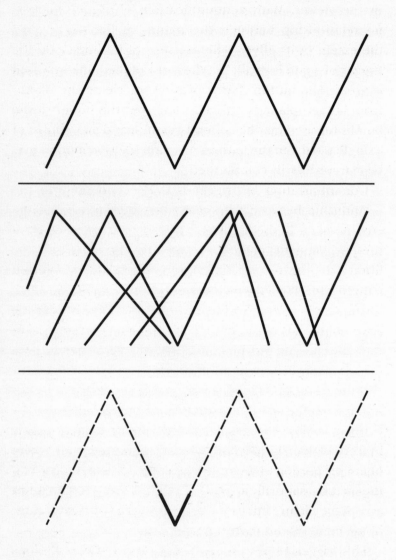

Fig. 34

in the viewer. With communication by trigger there is no relationship between the nature of the trigger and the extent of its effect. The pressure of the finger on the trigger of a gun is small, but the force of the bullet released is great. The button that is pressed to release the bombs from an aeroplane is a trivial thing, but the power of the bombs released may be colossal. A command may consist of a single word, but the pattern of action it sets in motion may be extraordinarily complicated.

Communication by trigger is the second stage in the relationship between the special memory-surface and the environment. In the first stage, patterns are extracted from the environment, made more definite and stored as in a library. In the second stage the appropriate established pattern appears on the memory-surface as soon as some identifying clue is offered by the environment. The clue may be a symbol or part of the pattern. The memory-surface elaborates the clue and provides the entire pattern, whether or not this is actually present in the environment – to such an extent that the pattern provided by the memory-surface may be different from the one that is available in the environment.

If you take a photograph of a man sitting in an armchair in front of you, his feet and legs may appear huge and quite out of proportion to the rest of him. The camera is recording the picture as it really appears. The mind, however, does not accept the picture but uses it to trigger off a standard picture of the man with his correct proportions.

This triggering process can obviously give rise to illusions and mistakes. These aspects will be considered later. Another effect of the use of ready-made patterns can be seen when such patterns are strung together, as in thinking. If these ready-made patterns are large, then the strung together sequence, like a ready-made suit of clothes, may not provide a good fit for the situation that is being thought about.

ELABORATION

Since the area of activation of the memory-surface has to reach a fixed size, any small pattern which is put onto the surface is expanded until this size is reached. If the pattern is too large, then it is of course cut down into attention areas.

Symbols are tiny patterns which can stand on their own. They may be part of a larger pattern, or they may be connected to it. They act as gateways to the larger pattern. In terms of the contours on the memory-surface they are the narrow entrances to valleys. Through them the flow can spread to cover the whole pattern. Though whole patterns may be much too large to be combined in a single area of activation, the much smaller symbols can be combined and still fall within the permitted area. From this combination may arise a new and useful pattern which can then have its own symbol. And so a hierarchy of new patterns can be formed by successive combinations of symbols. That is why language, and any form of symbolic representation, can help the processing of information. It is more convenient to use a symbol than to wait until a large pattern provides its own representative fragment.

The limited area of activation on the memory-surface might seem to provide little opportunity for elaboration of a presented pattern unless that pattern was very small. But since the area of activation can shift in a sequence of moves, the elaboration can be extensive. The position of the area at any one moment is determined by the contours of the surface. The movement of the area of activation from one place to another on the surface is determined by the tiring factor. The other factors may cause a permanent change in the contours through changes in the thresholds of the units; the tiring factor causes a temporary change in threshold, a temporary change in contour, which causes the area of activation to move on. Just as there is a definite pattern in space on the surface for a distinct input, so there can also be a definite sequence of patterns in time.

In this way, while retaining all the advantages of a limited area of attention, such as fragmentation and choice, the memory-surface also has the facility for unlimited elaboration by establishing fixed sequences of movement of attention as patterns in time. This interchangeability of time and space is an extremely useful information-processing characteristic of the surface. Established patterns may occur as a distribution of active units in space on the surface, or as a distribution in time, one set of units becoming activated after another.

CHAPTER 16

SHORT-TERM MEMORY

When you buy something in a shop and hand it to the shop assistant you remember the price of the object long enough to see that you get the right change. She in turn remembers what money you give her long enough to work out the right change. A few minutes later she will have forgotten this, and hours later you will have forgotten the price. If the cat has been sitting on your lap for some time and then, as all cats do, jumps down for no apparent reason, you may still feel the cat to be sitting there for some time after it has gone.

Short-term memory is the impression left by an event for a short while after it has gone. It is a sort of afterglow or shadow that lingers a bit longer than its cause. The short-term memory effect may become converted into a long-term memory effect, or it may disappear. Unless there is an actual conversion to a long-term memory effect the nature of the short-term memory effect is to disappear – but by then it may have served some purpose.

With the jelly model, the sculpting of the surface by the

hot water was a long-term, or permanent, memory effect. But if you actually tried out the jelly model instead of just reading about it you would notice a curious effect. If you place successive spoonfuls of hot water on the surface in such a way that each spoonful spreads into an area that is already wet, then a single network of channels forms on the surface. As a result, a spoonful of water placed anywhere on the surface will always find its way to the same spot. This always happens if you carry out the experiment in one session. If, however, you take several days over it, adding only a few spoonfuls each day, then the result is quite different. Although the spoonfuls may be placed in exactly the same positions and in exactly the same sequence as before, a single network does not appear. Instead several separate networks appear.

The explanation for this curious difference in behaviour of the jelly surface if the experiment is spread over several days lies in the way it dries out between sessions. No matter where the water actually goes, a spoonful of water always leaves a wet spot where it is first placed. Another spoonful placed alongside and spreading into this wet area will tend to flow into the wet area even if there is no significant depression. This is a surface-tension effect. The wetness of the surface constitutes a short-term memory of the placement of a spoonful of water. It makes it easier for water to flow into that area than into surrounding areas. If the wetness has dried out, then the second spoonful forms its own depression without flowing into and becoming part of the first network. This effect is shown on page 136.

The wetness of the jelly surface constitutes a short-term memory, and its effect is to unite things together into a single pattern, whereas without it separate patterns tend to form.

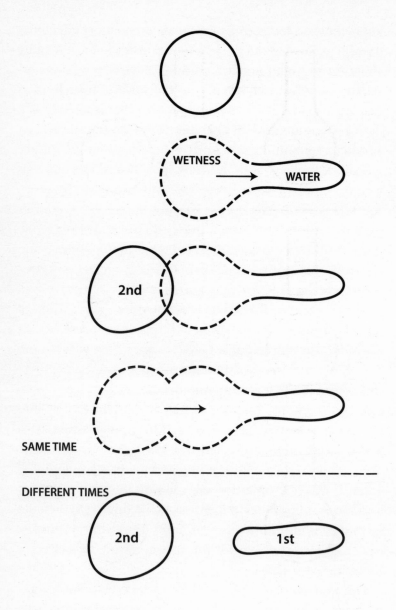

Fig. 35

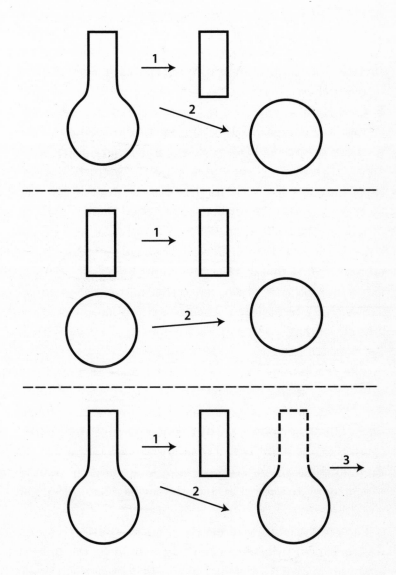

Fig. 36

SYNTHESIS

As we have seen, the major tendency of the special memory-surface is to break things up into separate fragments and to make these fragments as firm and distinct as possible. Fragmentation, separation, selection follow from the way the surface is organized. A large picture presented to the memory-surface is broken down into separate attention areas, each of which provides a specific pattern. Each of these patterns will leave its permanent effect on the surface. But as far as the surface is concerned there is nothing to tell whether the parts occurred together or as separate patterns presented on different days. This effect is shown on page 137. With a short-term memory effect each pattern leaves an afterglow which makes that part of the memory-surface easy to activate. From the combination of these afterglow areas a new pattern emerges as a synthesis of all the separate patterns.

A better example is provided by a huge picture filled with figures doing different things. One pays attention to the figures individually and sees what they are up to. As one's attention moves on to another part of the picture there remains a short-term memory of each figure, and in the end these are all synthesized into a complete pattern which comes to exist on its own. It may be a battle scene or a wedding feast.

The great usefulness of the recent memory effect is to put together again what has been fragmented by the limited attention span of the system. Things which existed as a whole can be recreated as a whole.

TIME AND SPACE

The limited attention span of the special memory-surface divides a large picture up into attention areas that are attended to one after another, so that what is spread out in space becomes spread out in time. As far as the memory-surface is concerned the picture might just as well have been spread out in time. A glass falling to shatter on the floor will be recorded as a sequence of patterns (glass in hand, glass falling, glass shattered, fragments). Whether the sequence of attention areas come from something that has been spread out in space or in time the effect is the same, and short-term memory acts to put the pieces together to enable a new composite pattern to emerge.

So far the short-term memory effect has only been considered as compensating for the limited attention span that breaks things up. But short-term memory can have a positive synthesizing effect that can create new patterns. If the attention area flits from part of one object to part of another, then those two parts may be combined to give a new pattern which only exists on the memory-surface. The pattern has been invented by the memory-surface. The same thing can happen with time. If two totally unconnected events follow upon each other, then the short-term memory effect can synthesize them into a pattern which again only exists on the memory-surface.

This synthesizing effect of short-term memory is the basis of association and learning. Teaching involves arranging an artificial but useful sequence so that short-term memory can create a pattern which links the things together permanently. A conditioned reflex is established in the same way.

Two unconnected events are put together time and again until, through short-term memory, a linking pattern develops to convert them into a single pattern.

HOLDING EFFECT

If the long-term memory effect is relatively slow, then short-term memory can serve to hold things around long enough for them to leave a long-term impression. This probably happens in the brain where long-term memory effects may involve chemical changes which take some time. Until this chemical change can be effected, the actual picture is preserved as electrical activity in the form of short-term memory. This system has obvious advantages in that short-term memory acts as a moving average which sorts things out before the long-term record is made. This is much more convenient than making the long-term record at once and then sorting things out.

SEPARATION AND SYNTHESIS

Breaking things down into units, establishing these units and then putting them together again in different combinations is what the special memory-surface does. The ability to do these things makes the memory-surface a powerful computing system. The combining property is common to most computing systems, but the unusual feature is the extracting and selecting property which allows the memory surface to organize its own input.

The separating behaviour of the memory-surface leads to discrimination and selection.

The combining behaviour of the memory-surface leads to association, learning and creation.

All this behaviour is really due to the self-organization of information in the ideal surroundings offered by the special memory-surface.

CHAPTER 17

The limited area of activation on the memory-surface is made up of the most excitable units so long as the result is a coherent pattern. High excitability means a low threshold for activation. When the surface is visualized as a jelly model where the area of activation flows to the lower part of the jelly surface, this can be taken as an area with a low threshold. When one is thinking of the columns on the tilting board, then one thinks in terms of high excitability, since the taller the column the more easily is it toppled over. High excitability or low threshold are interchangeable.

Various factors affect the excitability of the units. These factors have been introduced one by one and it might be useful to summarize them here. The most convenient model for this purpose is the tilting board with columns on it. Each factor affecting excitability alters the height of the columns. Some of these additions are permanent, some are temporary and some vary with time. Excitability at any particular moment is given by the height of the column at that moment.

1. If the pattern put onto the surface falls directly on a unit then that unit will have its excitability raised considerably.

2. A unit which is connected to an already activated unit will have its excitability raised. The more connections there are to already excited units the greater the rise in excitability.

3. Each time a unit is activated its excitability is permanently raised by an amount. In contrast to the first two effects, this is a permanent effect. In terms of the column model a new block is added to the height of the column each time it topples over.

4. After a unit has been activated there is a short-term memory effect and the unit remains more excitable for some time. This effect gradually wears off.

All the above effects raise the excitability of a unit. There are two further effects which lower the excitability of a unit.

5. An inhibiting influence which is proportional to the area of activation on the memory-surface decreases the excitability of each unit. (With the column model this is equivalent to the lesser degree of tilt that is required when some of the columns get taller.)

6. Immediately after a unit has been activated there is a sharp decline in excitability (tiring factor). This, however, soon recovers.

At first sight it may seem that the increased excitability of the short-term memory effect is incompatible with the tiring effect which makes an activated unit less excitable. The two effects can, however, be combined. On this page is shown a diagram representing the height of a column from moment to moment. A pattern falls on the unit, its excitability rises and it becomes activated. Then the tiring factor sets in and excitability is depressed below the resting level. The effect is transient and excitability rises to the short-term memory level which is above the resting level. This level slowly declines to a level which is permanently above the initial level.

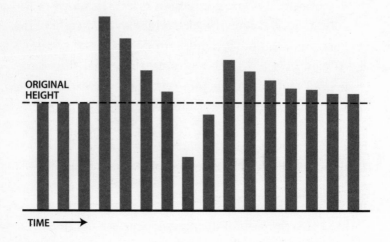

Fig. 37

In this example it is implied that the changes in excitability are all within the unit itself. They need not be, for they may be in the surroundings as well. Thus short-term memory may take the form of activity in connected units which makes it more likely for activity to return to the original unit. These different effects operating in each unit are sufficient to account for the position and movement of the limited area of activation. And the behaviour of this limited area of activation is sufficient to account for the information-processing carried out by the special memory-surface.

CHAPTER 18

In its handling of information the special memory-surface behaves as if it had a self. This self directs attention from one part of the environment to another, selecting some features and ignoring others. This self combines patterns together to create new ones that do not exist anywhere in reality, or takes a small pattern from the surroundings and extends it in an imaginative elaboration. This self has a unity of consciousness. And yet this is all due to the passive behaviour of information which is organizing itself on the special memory-surface.

In spite of having a self, the special memory-surface has no trace of selfishness. In fact the special memory-surface is saint-like in its selflessness. It is so unselfish that it would be extremely vulnerable and could never survive unless it was protected and its needs provided for. It never looks after its own interests because it is not yet aware of them. There is no special selection of those things which are necessary, nor is there any avoiding of those things that are harmful. Patterns are picked out of the environment solely on the basis of famil-iarity, and through such selection they become ever more familiar. Thus the knowledge or the content of the special memory-surface is determined entirely by the sequence of presentation of patterns to the surface and the repetition of them. In no way is this knowledge affected by the interests of the memory-surface itself. In the eyes of the special memory-surface all features of the environment are equally desirable and there is total impartiality in dealing with them. This could be a very inefficient system, for it would not enable a creature equipped with such a memory-surface to classify external features as helpful, harmful or indifferent.

So far the memory-surface has been considered as a disembodied information-handling device. The purpose of the book is essentially to deal with the information-handling (thinking) behaviour of such a memory-surface, but since this can be markedly affected by selfish interests it is necessary to consider these as well.

In order to supply the special memory-surface with selfish interests one has to supply it with some sort of body. This body is merely an organism that needs certain things from the environment for its survival. It also needs to avoid certain things for its survival. It is a matter of reactions to the environment and needs from the environment. The reactions, such as pain, are internal responses to an external event. The needs, such as hunger, are internal events that require an external response.

It is convenient to think of the memory-surface facing two environments at once (as on page 149). One environment is the ordinary external environment which is what the memory-surface has had to deal with so far. The other environment is provided by events within the body with which the memory-surface has been equipped. Both environments are capable of presenting patterns to the surface, but there is some difference in the sort of patterns that are presented. The internal environment presents patterns which reflect the state of the body, be it pain or hunger. As fixed patterns these tend to dominate the memory surface, persisting until the state of the body changes. Attention to them can fluctuate but it does not tend to move away from them entirely as it might from external patterns.

An event in the external environment can both imprint a pattern on the memory-surface and also affect the body in such a way that this also activates a pattern on the memory-surface. A syringe which caused a painful injection would be an example of such an event. The two patterns, syringe and pain, occurring in succession might link up, as might any two successive patterns on the memory-surface. Once the link had been established, the sight of the syringe might immediately give rise to fear, which would dominate the situation until the syringe was removed. This process is fairly straightforward and it does not exclude inbuilt or instinctual fears.

With the needs that arise within the body the situation is rather more complicated. A need such as hunger is evident as a pattern on the memory-surface. As a pattern it is vague and much less precise than the patterns that have been extracted from the external environment by the formalizing precision of the senses. Nevertheless the pattern is real and dominant on the surface. This pattern may have inbuilt connections to other patterns, and this would mean that if these other patterns were present in the environment then attention would settle on them. More usually, such connections are not inbuilt but have been built up by experience.

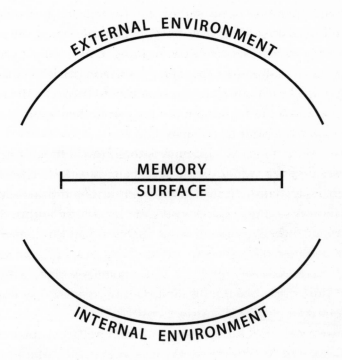

Fig. 38

If hunger were the need there might well be two associated patterns, each of which would depend on a different
state of the body. One pattern would be 'hunger need' and
the other would be 'hunger pleasure'. Any event which both
left a pattern on the memory-surface and also changed the
body so that the 'hunger pleasure' pattern was produced,
would become associated with the pleasure of relieving
hunger or eating. The two patterns would link up on the
surface through mechanisms described before. The 'hunger
need' pattern would also have to be connected up to the

149

'hunger pleasure' one in some way. Then the 'hunger need' would lead to those objects being selected which had been linked in the past with 'hunger pleasure'. Once again, if such links were firmly established then the external pattern alone might lead to the 'hunger pleasure' pattern being activated.

The actual mechanism for arousal, satisfaction or pleasure in connection with these internal needs is not important in this context. What is important is that these internally produced patterns intrude on the pure memory-surface and help to direct attention. Instead of the external information being left to self-organize on its own there is now an additional influence which picks out some things rather than others. Selection is no longer only on the basis of familiarity, but also on the basis of usefulness. There is still self-organization of information but the information now comes from both internal and external environments.

Since the internal environment can alter from moment to moment, depending on the chemical state of the body, the reaction to an external picture can also differ from one occasion to another. Whereas pure memory-surfaces faced with exactly the same sequence of external pictures would hold the same patterns, this could no longer be the case with selfish memory-surfaces, since the internal environments might be different. This makes for increased individuality.

The introduction of selfishness to the memory-surface adds a distorting factor to its information-handling. The memory-surface no longer deals with information for its own sake, but only in terms of its usefulness. In terms of survival or adaptation this may be essential. In terms of maximizing information this may be limiting.

Since the system is still a passive one, a certain pattern or idea can become dominant if it is connected to an internal pattern, that is, if it has an emotional bias. A connection then develops to link this dominant pattern with the initial presented pattern. Thus the conclusion is reached first and then rationalized back to the original situation. This is quite different from the developing of an initial pattern through a natural sequence of intermediate patterns to a final pattern. In this natural development, dominance depends on the sequence of patterns that have gone before and on accumulated experience.

CHAPTER 19

THE UNIVERSE OF THE SPECIAL MEMORY-SURFACE

In the previous sections the special memory-surface has been gradually built up, feature by feature, and its basic structure modified in a series of steps that made it more special each time. Nevertheless, at the end of these modifications the surface is still a relatively simple mechanical structure, with behaviour which is as determined by the nature of the structure as the behaviour of a dishwashing machine is determined by its design.

The behaviour of the special memory-surface is pretty effective. It can select and it can ignore. It can fragment into units or create new units out of fragments. It can extract patterns from confused material and it can abstract standard patterns from material that shows variation. It can represent complete patterns with a symbol and it can elaborate a symbol into a complete pattern. All this adds up to a remarkable information-processing system. But the system also has its limitations. These limitations are inseparable from the advantages, since they are the advantages looked at in a different way. For instance, the ability to establish firm patterns implies that changing a pattern may be very difficult. The ability actually to create new patterns means that these new patterns may be regarded as really existing in the environment when in fact they do not.

What happens on the special memory-surface happens in a universe that has very different rules of behaviour from the everyday universe. Just how different these rules are may be shown by supposing the special memory-surface to be a table top and the patterns presented to the surface to be objects put on the table. If a large object such as a large cereal packet were put on the table it would disappear, leaving behind a fragment of itself, such as the part bearing the label. Then that part would become ghostlike and another part would appear. This would be repeated until all the parts had appeared in turn, then suddenly the packet would shrink in size, lose its detail, but appear as one object.

If two dissimilar objects such as an egg and a piece of toast were placed on the table, then one or other would disappear. If one of these objects were already on the table, then addition of the other one would cause the first one to disappear, or it would itself disappear. Another possibility is that instead of disappearing, part of the egg and part of the piece of toast would join together to give half an egg on half a piece of toast. If both toast and egg were left on the table, then they might alternately appear and disappear until eventually a combined form appeared. If the toast were visible at any time then one would know that as one looked it would change into the egg, and the other way round.

The peculiar behaviour of the special universe of this table top is obviously quite different from the ordinary physical universe. In the ordinary universe one simply puts a poached egg on toast and it stays there without any strange behaviour. Ordinary addition means that when one thing is added to another the result is the sum of the two things. On the table top, however, the rules of addition are different. Here a sum is always exactly the same size as either one of the two parts which are themselves always of equal size. Indeed the sum would always be the same size no matter how many parts were added together. As well as this addition in space there would also be addition in time. This would mean that two things added together would result in one of them always being followed in sequence by the other.

It is not very useful to suppose that what happens on the special memory-surface is just a miniature version of what happens in the ordinary universe, translated into different units, just as the ordinary universe can be translated into patterns on a celluloid film or mathematical symbols. The special universe of the surface leads to totally different behaviour which can only be understood in terms of the rules of that universe.

CHAPTER 20

D-LINES

Patterns of light flickering across the surface of the thousand bulb model. Spoonfuls of water flowing over the surface of the jelly model. Both are visual illustrations of the way an activated area can flow over a memory-surface, picking out first one pattern then another, reacting to the environment or following its own sequence of flow. Once it is appreciated how the activated area arises and what it does then it is rather cumbersome to have to deal with whole models. It would be much more convenient to have some notation for dealing directly with the behaviour of activated areas.

A unique pattern presented to the special memory-surface will activate a unique area on that surface. A unique area is made up of a unique set of activated units which can be represented as points on the surface. On page 156 is shown an area that can be supposed to be made up of separate points. Each of these points is unique in that no other point has the same position on the page and exactly the same neighbours. This set of unique points represents the activated area on the memory-surface at any one moment. The unique group of points makes a unique pattern.

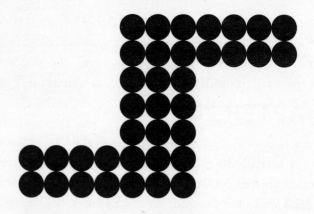

Fig. 39

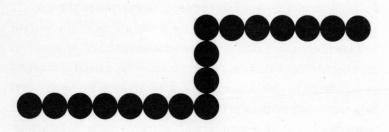

Fig. 40

But a unique set of points on the page does not have to be arranged as a compact area. They could be arranged as a thin strip or even as a single line of points and would be just as unique as a collection of points in the form of an area. If you draw a number of lines on a piece of paper, then each line is distinguishable from each other line because every one covers a unique set of points. There does not have to be a different shape to each line, it is the spatial position of the line that makes it unique. A straight line near the top of the page is quite different from a straight line half an inch farther down the page because they each cover a different set of points on the page. The whole page is taken as the memory-surface and each imaginary point on it is a unit. A line is drawn to connect units that have low thresholds and lie together in such a way that an area of activation would come to include them all. A line that does this may be called a d-line. Thus the d-line may represent an actual area of activation, but more often it represents a potential area of activation, an arrangement of low threshold units which tend to become activated as a whole. This would constitute an established contour on the surface, so in fact the d-lines do represent patterns recorded on the memory-surface.

The more often a unit is activated, the lower does its threshold become. This could be represented in d-lines by going over the same line again and again. This would not be very convenient as it would be impossible to tell just how often the line had been repeated. Instead, the repeat lines are shifted slightly to the side so that they become visible as lines parallel with and close to the original line. This is purely for the sake of convenience, as an actual line to the side would really cover different points. There is no need to draw a separate line for each time a particular pattern is activated. It is sufficient to use enough lines to show the relative degree of establishment among the patterns. As long as an order of preference among the patterns is clear then one, two or three lines will suffice. On page 158 are shown two d-line patterns, one of which is more familiar than the other and hence has an additional emphasis line alongside itself.

Fig. 41

Two separate patterns may have something in common. Using areas on a memory-surface, the two areas would overlap. This means that some points on the surface would be used by both areas, by both patterns. Exactly the same thing can be shown with d-lines. If any two points have been used by two patterns then the d-lines will overlap, since both patterns include these points. Since one cannot tell that one line is overlapping another, the second line is shifted so that it runs parallel to the first line but at a small distance from it. This is exactly the same procedure as for emphasis of a d-line.

As shown on page 159, emphasis of a d-line or overlap of two d-lines are both shown as a duplicated one. This is hardly surprising since overlap is itself an emphasis. Thus if a number of points have been used by two patterns then they are emphasized twice as much. So the areas of overlap do come to stand out on their own since they are repeated each time either of the two patterns is repeated.

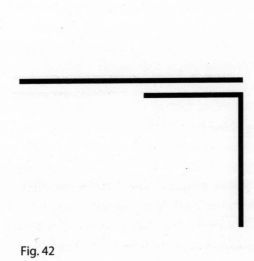

Fig. 42

Fig. 43

The attention span which represents the activated area on the memory-surface is limited, and so the length of d-line track that would be activated at any moment would also be limited. Each d-line fragment usually represents an attention span, an attention fragment. Where this is not the case, a light circle encloses the segment of line which does form the attention span.

Attention flows along the d-lines according to the rules of the memory-surface. These rules, which determine the movement of the activated area on the surface, include such things as the tiring factor which makes flow essential, and the established contours which decide where the flow goes. Contours, degree of emphasis, degree of establishment, low threshold, high excitability are all different ways of saying that some areas are preferred to others and flow is always towards such preferred areas.

If it is necessary to show that attention starts at a particular d-line fragment because a presented pattern is exciting that fragment, then a broken line may be shown alongside this fragment. This explains, for instance, the sequence of attention shown in the d-line diagram on page 159.

D-LINES AND BEHAVIOUR ON THE SPECIAL MEMORY-SURFACE

Some of the basic processes that occur on the special memory-surface can now be described, using the d-line notation.

FRAGMENTS AND CONTINUITY

The memory-surface breaks large pictures up into separate attention areas. Each of these attention areas can be considered as giving rise to a d-line fragment. On page 162 is shown a simple diagram of a picture which is broken up into two fragments, each of which results in a d-line. The two d-lines overlap. If the same picture occurs again and again then both d-lines come to be emphasized together, and a fixed sequence of attention is established, so that attention always moves from one to the other. This fixed sequence of attention flow virtually converts the two separate d-lines into a single line, since the movement of attention may be extremely rapid. The more often the figure occurs as a whole, and the more the d-lines are emphasized as a sequence, the more they stand out from other patterns so that attention flow elsewhere is less and less likely. Thus although the original picture was divided into two fragments, it still comes to be treated as a complete picture because the sequence of attention flow becomes fixed.

If, however, the same picture was not repeated by itself but interspersed with other patterns, as shown on page 163, then one part of the pattern would get emphasized much more than the other part and would develop as a unit on its own. The flow of attention would not be as fixed as before, and the original picture might come to be regarded as an assembly of two separate parts rather than as a whole. The d-lines shown in (a), (b) and (c) indicate how emphasis on part of the pattern tends to separate this out as a unit on its own.

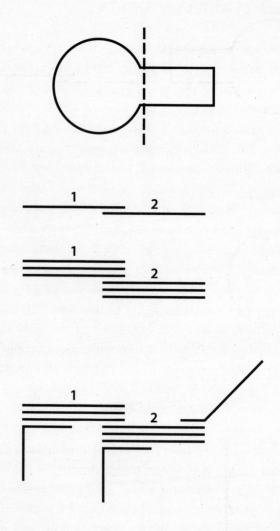

Fig. 44

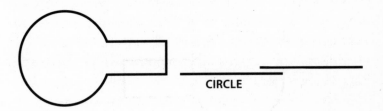

Fig. 45a

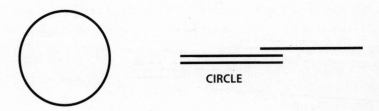

Fig. 45b

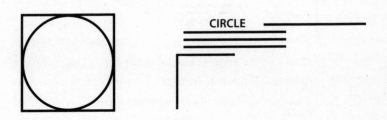

Fig. 45c

Thus, whether a large picture comes to be regarded as a whole or as an assembly of separate units depends on the repetition of the picture as a whole and the occurrence of other distracting patterns which emphasize only some of the units. There is a danger in regarding a complete picture as an assembly of arbitrary attention units, for this can prevent the picture being looked at in another way. There is the opposite danger when an assembly of units occurs so often as a whole that it comes to be regarded as a natural whole which cannot be split up into its component parts. The memory-surface does not distinguish between true parts and parts created by the attention system. Nor does it distinguish between true wholes and wholes created by the combining function of fixed attention sequences.

DIVERSION

If a fixed sequence of attention units develops as a pattern, then this fixed sequence can divert the attention flow of any lesser pattern that leads into it. On page 166 is shown a pattern that might have developed on the memory-surface. If, however, a stronger pattern is already present on the surface, then the flow of attention is diverted by the stronger pattern and the weaker one never gets established. An example of this sort is given by my failure to notice the peculiar tops to the traffic lights in Marylebone. Looked at as a metal object, the traffic light standard does have a peculiar top; near the top there happens to be a light. That is the pattern that might be established by someone who knew nothing about traffic lights. The actual light is the area of overlap. Unfortunately this light is part of a stronger pattern which has to do with driving a car. The importance of the light for this purpose is more dominant than a mere aesthetic interest in street furniture. Attention is led away along this better emphasized pattern, and as a result the peculiar tops to the standards are never noticed.

CENTRING

This process is very similar to that of diversion, but more complete. If a new pattern falls athwart an established pattern, then the new pattern may never become established on its own. The situation giving rise to the new pattern will tend to be seen in terms of the old pattern. On page 167 is shown a new pattern as it might have become established had there not already existed another pattern. But there is an established pattern, so instead of becoming established on its own the new pattern serves to re-emphasize the old one. This is why some things may be very easy to understand at the time but impossible to remember afterwards.

The great usefulness of centring is that a definite pattern can be established from a series of patterns that are no more than roughly similar. This definite pattern is not, however, a true average of the variations since it is much affected by which of the variations came first.

POLARIZING

The same process that gives rise to centring and diversion also gives rise to polarizing. Polarizing occurs when the

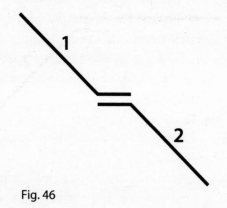

Fig. 46

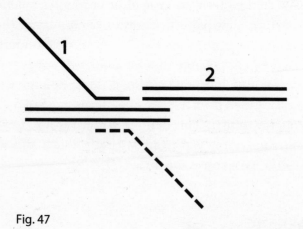

Fig. 47

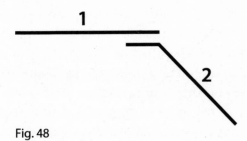

Fig. 48

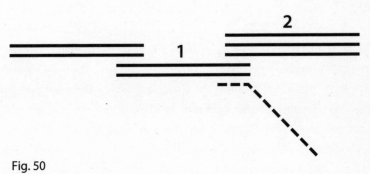

Fig. 49

Fig. 50

presented picture, instead of being broken down into its natural attention areas, is broken down into already established units. The effect is illustrated with d-lines on page 169. The natural breakdown of a presented picture into attention units is shown in (a). When ready-made units are available, as in (b), then the breakdown takes advantage of these units and a new attention area must be created as a link between them. Since this link is so much weaker than the ready-made units, the original picture comes to be regarded as a chance combination of the two ready-made units.

The danger is not just that the ready-made units may not be the most appropriate for the situation, but also that these units themselves lead off to other patterns which only serve to make the artificial split even wider. Once again this polarizing process is both a disadvantage and an advantage. Without these pre-formed ready-made units it would be difficult to recognize and react to new situations. Ready-made units are especially useful for quick action.

UNIT SIZE

With time, the ready-made units that are established on the memory-surface get larger and larger. Since the size of the limited area of activation on the memory-surface is fixed by the mechanics of the surface, neither this nor the area of attention ever get larger. Repetition of sequences of attention fragments establishes patterns which are large and fixed. These fixed sequences function as single units, even though they involve several attention areas and even though they may be embedded in other patterns (as shown on page 169).

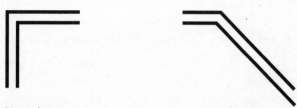

Fig. 51a

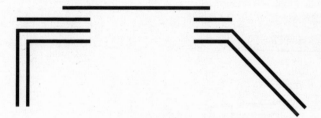

Fig. 51b

Fig. 51c

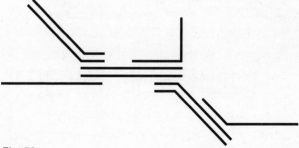

Fig. 52

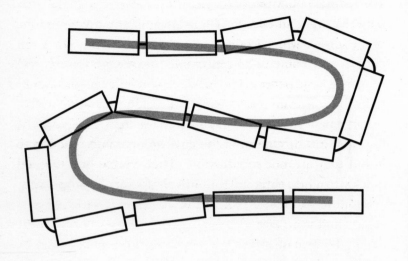

Fig. 53

Fig. 54

The natural behaviour of the memory-surface is to make such patterns larger and larger. There is nothing in the behaviour of the surface which would tend to break them up. The large pattern may come to be represented by a symbol but it still remains a large pattern. Once there is symbolic representation then there is even less chance of breaking up the pattern.

Large patterns are very much more use than small patterns for rapid interpretation of the environment and reaction to it, but they are not very flexible. They enable one to react quickly to a new situation, but not always very appropriately.

Suppose you had a string of beads, as in a necklace or a rosary, and were trying to arrange this string of beads to fit a design drawn on a piece of paper as shown on page 170. If the beads were small, then you would get a much better fit than if they were large. An assembly of small units will always give a better match than an assembly of large units.

ABSTRACTION

Abstraction seems to require the conscious picking out of some feature that is common to several different patterns. In fact, abstraction is the natural behaviour of the special memory-surface, and it is quite passive. Since features which are identical come to occupy the same position on the memory-surface, any feature that is common to different pictures will be emphasized each time one of the pictures occurs. So a feature which occurs in four separate pictures will be emphasized four times as strongly as the rest of the picture. In this way common features extract themselves. The usefulness of this from an information-processing point of view is great.

STARTING-POINT AND SEQUENCE OF ATTENTION

With the d-line notation attention always flows onto the more heavily emphasized d-line fragment. (This is equivalent to the area of activation on the memory-surface moving to the area with the lowest threshold units.) This means that without any change in the actual d-line diagram, the flow of attention can be quite different if it starts at a different place. This different starting place could be due to a presented pattern or to a different entry into the d-line pattern from the preceding pattern. On this page and opposite is shown a d-line diagram in which the actual flow of attention is quite different if the starting-point is different. The different attention sequences end up at different places. This implies that even if the features of a situation are not altered, the order in which these features are paid attention may make a big difference to the result. This phenomenon is the basis of most arguments between people.

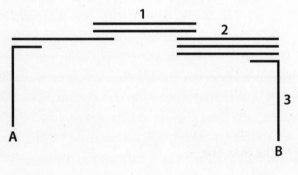

Fig. 55

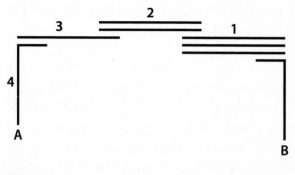

Fig. 56

SUMMARY

The d-lines provide a convenient notation for describing what can happen on the special memory-surface. The d-lines indicate emphasis and connections, and from these is derived attention flow. Attention flow is a very important part of information-processing, and probably the basis of learning. Attention flow is also thinking.

Different aspects of the behaviour of the special memory-surface can be described with the help of d-lines. The d-lines do not prove anything, but merely provide a more convenient method of description than words. There are occasions, however, when the behaviour of the d-lines themselves may suggest a type of behaviour that might be expected to occur on the special memory-surface. This can then be examined further for its own sake.

PART 2

CHAPTER 21

On page 178 are shown a selection of unusual and very unlikely shapes for the front wheel of a bicycle. By carefully examining the characteristics of these shapes one would be able to predict what sort of ride one would have on a bicycle equipped with any one of these wheels. The performance of the system is determined by the nature of the system. It would be very surprising if a bicycle with square wheels gave you a smooth ride, just as it would be surprising if a bicycle with round wheels gave you a jerky ride.

Part One has been used to describe the nature of the system called the special memory-surface. This is equivalent to examining the bicycle wheel, and getting a general idea of its shape. The next step is to use this shape to work out how the system would work. One ought to be able to predict the sort of behaviour that should occur. One might also be able to explain the behaviour that does occur. Finally, one might be able to devise ways of altering the behaviour. Of particular use is the realization that there are inherent disadvantages in the system.

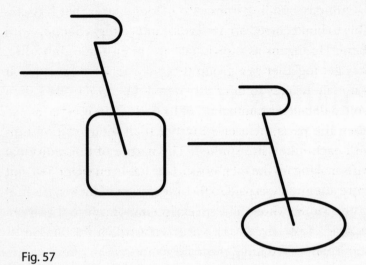

Fig. 57

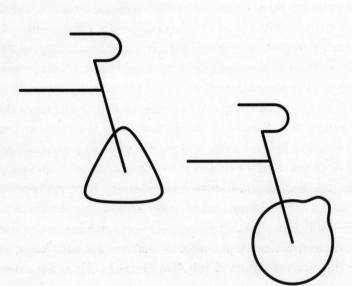

Fig. 58

Ordinary building bricks are oblong blocks, but it is possible to build curved arches and round factory chimneys with them. Hooligans as individuals are often timid, but when they get together as a group they may be very aggressive. It is not always easy to infer the over-all behaviour of a system from a detailed examination of its parts. This is especially so when the parts themselves, rather than their relationships with each other, are studied. The nature of the individual parts making up the memory-surface has been examined, but more attention was paid to the integration of these parts into a functioning whole. The special memory-surface is a system capable of certain types of behaviour which depend on its organization and not just on the nature of the parts.

There are certain broad types of behaviour that are made inevitable by the nature of the special memory-surface system. For instance, in such a system it would be very unlikely for patterns to become less and less rigid. The whole system is geared to establishing patterns ever more firmly, to making pattern units larger and larger, to making paths deeper and deeper. The special memory-surface is nothing more than an opportunity for information to organize itself. It would be rather surprising if in such a self-organizing system the information became less and less organized.

I once watched a circus act in which a beautiful girl rode into the ring on a gold-plated bicycle. She then proceeded to strip the bicycle into pieces while still riding round on it. Eventually she was just riding on the back wheel alone. In the course of this elegant performance the girl rode for much of the time with the front wheel off the ground. There are many expert cyclists who could do this. If you were to ride around on the back wheel of a bicycle, then the shape of the front wheel would no longer determine the nature of the ride. So the misshapen front wheels offered earlier would no longer have any effect.

Bricks may be oblong, but if you choose to build a round factory chimney with them then it can be done. Perhaps it is not the system that determines what happens but only how the system is used. If you have a bicycle with a square front wheel but choose to ride on the back wheel only, then the actual shape of the front wheel will not affect the outcome. So perhaps the nature of the memory-surface does not determine what happens on it.

You can fry an egg in a pan, or scramble it, or make an omelette. You can choose what to do with the egg-pan-fire system. But there has to be a separate 'you' outside the system who decides what to do. Left to itself, the system will behave in a characteristic way according to its nature. The point about the special memory-surface is that it does not need to be manipulated from outside, but functions entirely from within itself. If it gives the illusion of being organized by a separate self, that is because it is self-organizing and the choice and attention directing appear to be active and not passive.

If one prefers to feel that the memory-surface is only being manipulated by some other information-processing agency there remains the question of how the other agency itself works. This book is only concerned with the behaviour of the special memory-surface which allows information to organize itself. An outside manipulating agency is not required for this system, but not thereby excluded. The emphasis in the book is on information-processing. At first the memory-surface is concerned with extracting definite patterns from a confused environment and establishing these patterns. Once this has happened then the memory-surface only needs a clue from the environment to call forth the already established patterns. The two processes are not distinct or separate. There is always a balance between the two. The balance may be one way or the other.

THINKING BEHAVIOUR ON THE SPECIAL MEMORY-SURFACE

What sort of thinking results from the way the special memory-surface is organized? What is the special behaviour that arises from the nature of this special type of system? The system does have a characteristic behaviour, and this has advantages and disadvantages. The disadvantages are inseparable from the advantages since they both arise from the same process. The bright plumage of a bird may make it more attractive to its mate and easier for it to find, but it also makes it more conspicuous for a predator.

The natural behaviour of the system will be discussed first, and then the limitations that are implicit in that natural behaviour will be made more explicit.

The reaction of the memory-surface to a picture that is presented to it has been the main subject of consideration so far. Patterns have been treated as direct reactions to the presented picture just as a photograph is a direct reaction to the scene in front of the camera. But once patterns have become established on the memory-surface then there is much that happens on the memory-surface that is not a direct reaction to a presented picture. A presented picture may set off a flow of activation across the surface, and this flow may lead on to other things quite far removed from the picture. The flow can proceed from place to place and back again without the need for pictures to be presented to the memory-surface in order to keep things going. This flow across the memory-surface could be called thinking. The most important point to keep in mind is that the special memory-surface is a passive mechanical system. It never actually does anything. Information moulds the contours of the surface and attention flows over these contours as water flows over uneven ground, now this way, now that way, pausing and flowing. The water leaves its track on the ground but the ground does not bestir itself to direct the water.

It was fashionable at one time to try to describe the building blocks of thought processes. It was supposed that the mind assembled images or concepts in order to think. Attention was supposed to be directed from one image to another in order to establish a pathway for thought. On the special memory-surface images are not the building blocks of thought. Nor do they influence the flow of thought in any way. The images are merely indications that the flow of activation has paused long enough to give an image. The image no more directs the flow of activation than the sight of a train at the station directs the route of that train.

On page 183 is shown a carpet-like surface which bears a number of depressions. Water is placed in the first depression and the edge of the carpet is lifted slowly as shown. The water will be forced to move across the surface of the carpet. It will pause in a depression, then move to an adjacent depression, then move without pause to a distant depression. This is the way the area of activation moves across the special memory-surface. Sometimes the pauses are linked to each other and there appears to be a succession of images. At other times there is a gap, as the flow moves without pause to a distant image. At other times the activation may die out in one area and start up again in a completely different area instead of actually moving across to that area. This sort of behaviour follows directly from the way the surface is organized.

For the sake of convenience, the pathway of the flow of thought described in this book will usually be taken as a series of linked images as indicated by d-lines which connect up with each other. This in no way excludes the occurrence of non-sequential images or even imageless thought.

Fig. 59

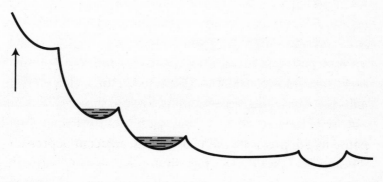

Fig. 60

CHAPTER 22

THINKING

Rather than constantly referring back to the flow of an activated area from one part of the memory-surface to another, from this point thinking behaviour will be discussed solely in terms of d-line diagrams. Thinking is the flow of attention along the d-line pathways.

This simple statement implies two things. First, that there are d-line pathways already established, and second, that there are some rules which govern flow. According to this idea, thinking cannot by itself establish new pathways but can only follow the ones that are already there. The sequence of flow or even the direction of flow may come to be altered, but the basic pathways remain the same. The way the pathways can be altered is considered in a later section. This section deals with flow along established pathways.

Many narrow roads in England suddenly open up into wide dual carriageways. Flow along the dual carriageway is swift and easy. Then after a few hundred yards or perhaps even a few miles the dual carriageway stops and it is a narrow road again. Similarly, with the d-line pathways there are parts which are firmly emphasized and which stand out as separate units. Once one enters such a unit then flow is swift and sure right to the end of it. The whole d-line pattern may be considered as a number of such units connected together by less well-established pathways. With time, the units tend to get larger and larger as the connecting paths are better established and separate units become linked together to make larger units. Nevertheless, the units do not lose their identity in the process, for any emphasis which establishes the connecting pathway also establishes the original units more firmly. This process is shown on page 186, where two separate units come together to form one larger background unit but remain separate in themselves. As suggested earlier, this tendency of units to get bigger makes the pattern of thought flow less flexible.

Selection, choice, preference, are characteristic of the activated area on the memory-surface, and therefore of the attention span and of thought flow along the d-lines. Actually the path selects itself. But it is more convenient (so ego orientated are we) to talk of flow selecting a path.

Even along a basic d-line pattern the direction of the flow can vary in two ways. It can vary as to the path it takes whenever there is a choice of direction. It can vary as to the actual sequence in which the different d-line fragments are covered. What factors determine the choice of pathway?

The first factor is familiarity – how well the d-line has been emphasized. This is the long-term memory effect, the permanently lowered threshold. The second factor is the pathway that has been followed up to the point in question. This pathway gives the sequence of attention areas, the context. For a particular path to be followed it helps for it

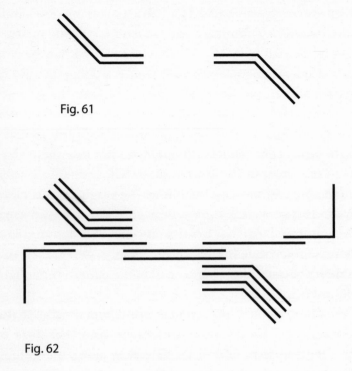

Fig. 61

Fig. 62

to lie in the line of flow. Short-term memory and the tiring factor can also affect whether a particular pathway is more likely or less likely to be followed. Finally, relevance to an internal need will be an overriding factor whenever an internal pattern is operating.

On the whole the two things that affect choice of path are the degree of establishment of that path through repetition and the sequence of flow. This is shown on page 188. In picture (a) the attention sequence follows the better emphasized of two possible pathways. In pictures (b) and (c) the attention sequence follows first one pathway and then the other, depending on the starting-point of the sequence. In both cases it ends in the same place, but if the link marked (Y) were missing it would end in a different place.

How much difference does there have to be between two alternative pathways for one of them to be chosen? As suggested earlier, the slightest difference will suffice. This follows from the self-maximizing behaviour of the memory-surface. Whether the difference in attractiveness between two pathways is huge or minimal does not make any difference. The pathway with the advantage will be chosen. The only importance of the size of the difference is that a huge difference is likely to be more durable than a slight difference which might be reversed by a change in some of the circumstances.

The obvious advantage of this system, which can make a choice on a minimal difference, is that selection of a pathway will always be definite, and the system cannot be blocked through being unable to choose between two almost equal pathways. Another advantage is that if a temporary difference makes one pathway preferable to another, then the mere use of the pathway will enhance the difference and so increase it. Thus slight differences are magnified. The disadvantage of the system is that alternatives which are very nearly as probable as the chosen pathway will be as ignored as if they were very different. It is like coming second in the hundred-metres race by only 0.1 seconds, or in the mile by a mere matter of two feet after having run over five thousand feet. But second it is, and the winner alone is recognized. In the d-line diagram shown on page 188, the merest difference in establishment between A and B will cause the flow to move off along B, and path A will be completely ignored.

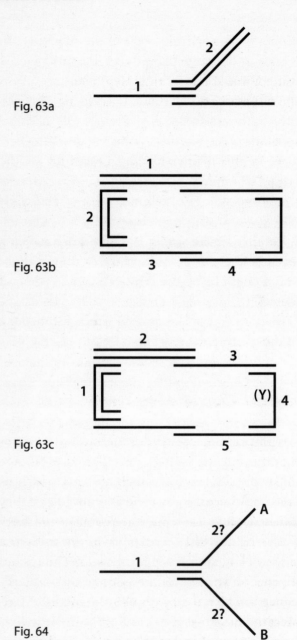

Fig. 63a

Fig. 63b

Fig. 63c

Fig. 64

SUMMARY

The interesting points about this thinking behaviour of the system may be summarized:

1. That thinking cannot of itself establish new pathways.
2. That with time the units tend to get larger and less flexible.
3. That the entry point into a pathway may make a great difference to the direction of flow.
4. That the slightest difference is sufficient for selection of a pathway.

These points do not completely cover behaviour of the system, but they pick out several interesting things that follow directly from the nature of the system.

CHANGES IN ESTABLISHED PATTERNS

Thought flow through a particular path does not basically change that path but tends rather to reinforce it. How then do the established patterns, the established pathways, the d-line diagrams, ever become changed?

The established patterns represent the natural development of a pattern. They come about through the self-organization of information as it comes in. The chance nature of the encounter with certain types of situation, the chance sequence in which the pieces of information are collected, all affect the development of the established pattern. For this reason the natural pattern may not be the best one.

That is where learning and education come in – as attempts to change the natural pattern into a better one. By what processes are the natural patterns altered?

EXTENSION

The simplest change in a d-line diagram would be by extension. On page 191 is shown part of a d-line diagram which is simply extended by addition of a further attention fragment. In practical terms the juxtaposition of a new pattern (E) just after the pattern shown in the d-line diagram (A) would result in the two being linked up through the short-term memory effect. The link-up may be effected at once or it may require a number of repetitions. The process is one of simple extension, of simple addition learning. It is rather like knowing that there is a bush at the bottom of the garden, and that there are bright berries on the bush. One day you pick a berry and find it tastes nice. The pattern of the garden and the bush and the berries is now extended to include the taste of the berry. It is rather like working in a large office and repeatedly noticing an attractive blonde girl in the canteen at lunch time. Then one day you find out her name. Another day you find out where she works. And so on. The pattern extends gradually.

DIVERSION

If all learning were a matter of simple extension then education would be merely a matter of providing opportunity for simple extension to build up the most useful patterns. The availability of certain patterns would be carefully contrived, but nothing else. Unfortunately it may be necessary to alter the natural pattern that has evolved. So it becomes not just a matter of extension but of diversion. In a sense, diversion is no more than extension in the face of competition. In the d-line diagram on page 193 natural flow would follow the sequence shown. Learning would involve an alteration in this pattern so that flow would follow the broken line instead.

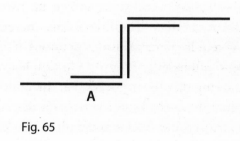

Fig. 65

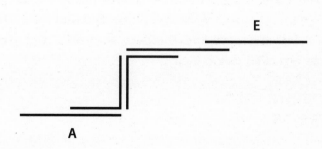

Fig. 66

It is not easy to bring about this diversion because one cannot just repeat the original pattern and tack a bit onto it as with simple extension. Each repetition of the original pattern would strengthen the wrong pathway, and so make the diversion ever more difficult.

One can make use of the dominance of internal patterns on the memory-surface to block the natural pathway as shown in picture (c) on page 194. This would involve fear or punishment, and the actual way this works will be discussed later. As a method, this would be rather ineffective. It might serve to block a whole pathway, but would be unlikely to block just part of a pathway. The other alternative is to use some positive internal pattern to attract attention to the diverging pathway in the hope that this will then link up with the main pathway. This leads on to an interesting point that is suggested by the d-line notation.

As shown in picture (e) on page 194, it should be easier to link up the new pathway if one actually starts with that pathway and then works backwards than if one starts at the beginning and works forwards.

In a way, positive emphasis of the divergent pathway is a method of working backwards, since attention is directed first to the new and emphasized fragment and then to the path by which it may be reached.

PREFERENCE

This is a special example of the diversion process. In this case the pathway is already established, but less well than an alternative pathway. The task is to emphasize the unused pathway so that it can take over. Once again, repetition of the whole pattern would tend to emphasize the wrong pathway. The same comments apply here as apply to the diversion process. There is, however, one point that is different. The diversion pathway could be built up separately and then an attempt made to link it up to the main pattern. The unused pathway cannot be built up separately as it is already part of the pattern.

All these methods of changing the basic established pattern are gradual. They usually require frequent repetition before the link-up is established. But what about those instances in which learning occurs suddenly, in a sort of snap fashion? How does this insight type of change in the established pattern come about?

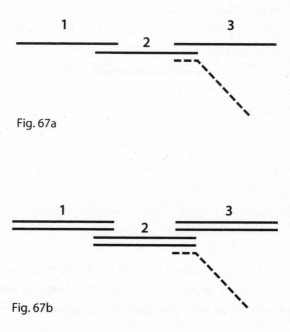

Fig. 67a

Fig. 67b

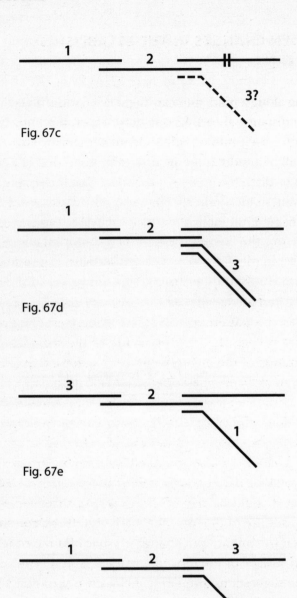

Fig. 67c

Fig. 67d

Fig. 67e

Fig. 67f

SUDDEN CHANGES IN THE ESTABLISHED PATTERN

Driving along a road, one may vaguely see some object on the road a distance ahead. As one gets nearer, the object seems to resolve itself into a road accident with a car in the ditch. Then all of a sudden the picture changes to that of a tractor digging a ditch by the side of the road. The interesting point is the very sudden switch from one interpretation to another. The image of the object on the road sets off an elaboration pattern on the memory-surface. Then the image changes slightly and there is a shift to a completely different pattern.

It is not very difficult to understand how a change in a picture presented to the memory-surface can lead to a sudden change in the pattern it evokes. The suddenness of the switch-over just reflects the flip-flop nature of the self-maximizing organization of the memory-surface. A pattern that becomes slightly more likely will suddenly become most likely.

What is rather more difficult to understand is how there can be a sudden and complete change in interpretation without any change whatsoever in the picture. On pages 196–197 is shown a pattern of lines inscribed like a flower in a hexagon. But if you look hard enough at this pattern you may suddenly see that it could be regarded as a pile of three cubes with the top surface of the top cube marked A. If you continue to look at it you might see it change to a pile of three cubes with the top surface of the top cube marked B. It may be argued that the suggestions given here are really responsible for the switch over but this can in fact occur without any such instructions. How is it that exactly the same presented picture can lead to such different elaboration patterns?

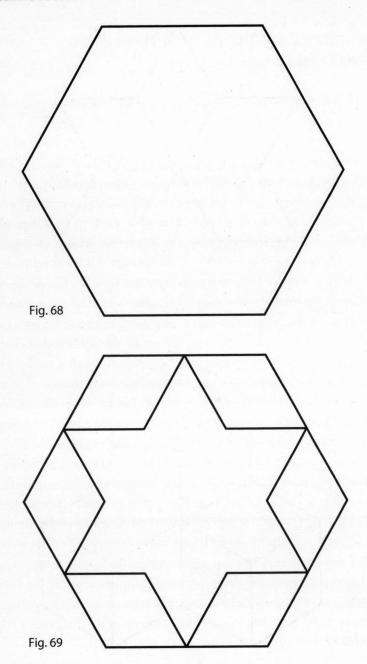

Fig. 68

Fig. 69

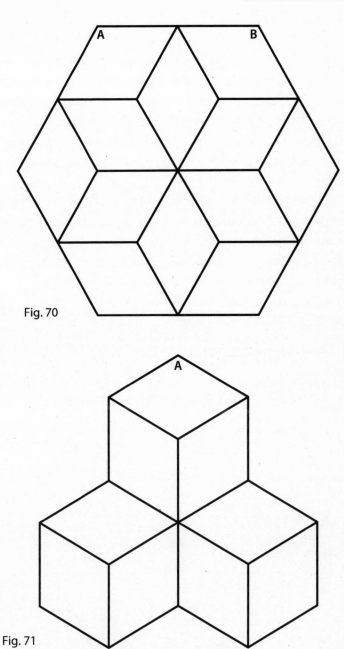

Fig. 70

Fig. 71

Solution to a difficult problem may suddenly come about through a flash of insight in a eureka moment. There may be no new information, but the whole thing may suddenly re-structure itself to give a completely different pattern. Could this sort of thing occur on the special memory-surface? If the thought flow does not actually alter the d-line pattern, then how can a new pattern emerge simply as a result of thought flow?

The interesting thing is not only that a new pattern emerges quite suddenly, without any apparent change in the external situation, but that it at once becomes permanent. This is peculiar in view of the gradual nature of the other methods of changing the basic pattern.

CHAPTER 23

INSIGHT

There are two convenient models of the insight situation. The first model involves what might be called short-circuiting. A long and tedious way of carrying out some task suddenly gives way to a quick and neat way of doing it. Once this has come about it is so obvious that everyone exclaims, 'Of course, why didn't we think of that before?' It is rather like driving to a favourite restaurant by a long, roundabout route. Suddenly you realize that if you go through a side street the restaurant is within walking distance of your home anyway. The second model is the eureka situation. A problem has been impossible to solve. Then suddenly in a flash of insight and without any further information the solution becomes clear. Both these examples could occur quite easily on the special memory-surface.

The short-circuiting situation is shown in a d-line diagram on page 201. The sequence of attention areas is shown starting at position (A) and following all round the circuit to reach the completed task at position (B). There are nine steps from start to completion. This sequence is inevitable, since the flow of attention must always be towards the better established d-line fragment. Thus from (A), flow must go towards (C), and once at (C) it must proceed around the whole circuit. (It cannot just flow back again because of the tiring factor, without which there would never be any flow at all.)

In the second d-line diagram on page 201 the layout is exactly the same, but this time the sequence is only three steps long instead of nine. A short circuit has occurred. Exactly the same d-line fragments are present, with exactly the same degree of emphasis. How has this short circuit, or flash of insight, come about? The explanation is surprisingly simple. If the first attention area is (C), then flow has to be towards (A), since this is better established; and once at (A), flow continues directly to (B). It is all a matter of the first attention area.

In the above example a flash of insight has come about simply as a result of looking at one part of the problem before another. A very slight shift in attention can make this huge difference. The emphasis is on slight. How then does this slight shift in attention come about?

The d-line diagram shown on page 201 would never stand in isolation, it would follow on from flow along some other d-line pattern, and this flow would then lead in to the pattern shown. Depending on what the previous patterns were, the flow might lead into the pattern shown at either (A) or (C). The usual entry point would be (A), but if one day because one had been thinking of something quite different the entry point were (C), then the flash of insight would occur. It would be inconceivable that the whole sequence of thought before the problem was arrived at should be absolutely identical on every occasion. On the other hand, insight is not frequent because a dominant entry point may remain the same even though the preceding patterns are different.

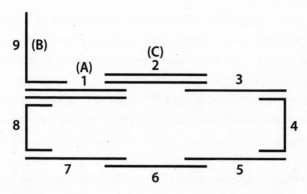

Fig. 72

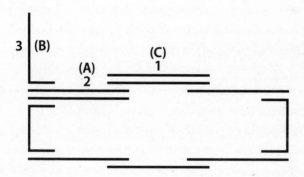

Fig. 73

The change in entry point to the d-line diagram of the problem could also come about through a change in internal patterns. Some mood or motivation change could emphasize some part of a preceding pattern more than usual, and this would lead to an unusual entry point. An external object present at the time, or before, could also affect the entry point. Archimedes splashing around in his bath had the entry point altered by the idea of water. Newton walking in the garden had the entry point changed by the apple that dropped on his head. These are trivial things in themselves, but if they serve to change the entry point into the problem sequence then they can set off a flash of insight.

The three important points about the insight phenomenon are as follows:

1. The problem sequence itself (i.e. the information available) remains completely unchanged.
2. A different entry point into this sequence can change the outcome markedly.
3. The change in entry point can come about for trivial unconnected reasons that affect not the problem itself but what has gone before.

Once the solution has been reached on one occasion why should it remain permanent? Here one might consider the peculiar pleasure that accompanies a 'snap' or insight type solution. Once the answer is known, then attention shifts from the starting-point of the problem to the end point. Starting at the end point one works backwards, and then there is no difficulty about sequences. One could also say that every slight initial difference which brought about the different entry point could be slightly reinforced by the pleasure of solution, and so become the usual entry point. With time, the pathway would become established as the dominant one. It is important to remember that insight solutions can be forgotten, just as jokes can. One is left with a vague feeling that it can be done, but does not quite remember how.

Another insight situation is shown as a d-line diagram on

this page. In the top diagram the thought flow chases round and round in a circle. By the time the flow returns to the starting-point the tiring factor has worn off so it can take that path again. Without any change in the d-line pattern, but with a change in the entry point to the sequence, the

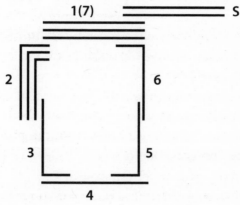

Fig. 74

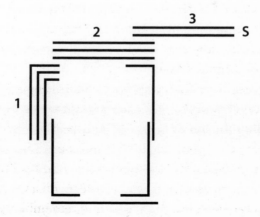

Fig. 75

flow escapes from the circular trap and quickly reaches (S), which is the solution point. This is not an example of short-circuiting but of a problem which did not have a solution. A slight change in the entry point into the sequence suddenly produces a solution.

If you give a person a postcard and a pair of scissors and ask him to cut a hole in the postcard big enough to put his head through, a curious thing often happens. You explain to him that a hole is space surrounded by continuous postcard without any joins. (Those who wish to try it for themselves could pause here.)

Most people start to cut into the postcard and then around it to make a spiral as shown on page 206. They either finish the spiral or give up as soon as they realize that they will end up with something that has two ends. They then discard the spiral and start again on a fresh postcard.

The fascinating point is that they were so near to solution with the spiral but could not get there. All one needs to do is to regard it not as a spiral but as a long strip. If one were asked to make a hole in a long strip one would at once cut it down the middle. This is shown for the postcard spiral on page 207. The hole that results is easily big enough to put one's head through.

This postcard situation is shown in d-line form on page 208. One starts off with the postcard and then has some vague notion of a thin rim of postcard. This leads on to the spiral effort. Once the spiral is achieved this leads very strongly to the two-end realization and the path is blocked. When it is pointed out that a spiral is also a strip then solution follows. In remembering the solution one then works back from the slit in the strip to the spiral as a strip-producing method.

Fig. 76

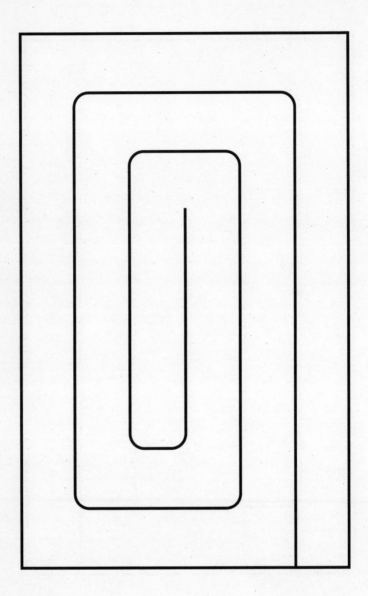

Fig. 77

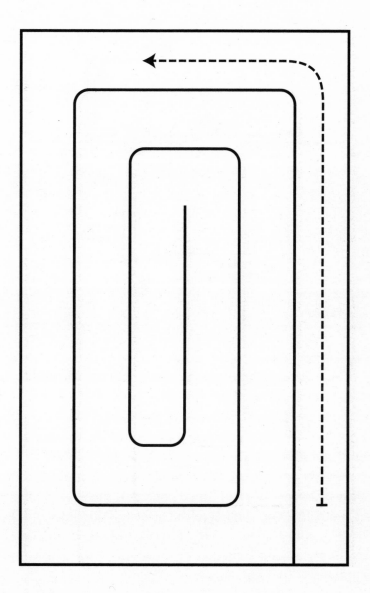

Fig. 78

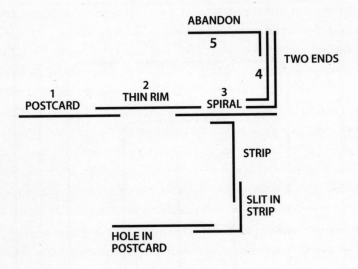

Fig. 79

If one were to put down the spiral cut postcard and then pick it up again later one might be more able to see it as a strip than as a spiral. The interesting thing is that onlookers who have not been concerned in cutting out the spiral are more apt to see it as a strip and to reach the solution.

It might be suggested that there was a switch point at the d-line fragment marked 'spiral', and that there was a choice of two paths, one leading to the 'two-end' difficulty and the other leading to the 'strip'. Some emphasis at this point might have been sufficient to cause the 'strip' path to be chosen and the problem solved.

Undoubtedly this type of problem-solving does also occur on the special memory-surface. Whenever there is a choice point and the difference in emphasis between the two alternative routes is slight, then a slight change in emphasis may suddenly make solution possible. This very slight change in emphasis may come about for a variety of reasons, including emotional changes or use of that d-line segment by another pattern recently enough for the short-term memory facilitation to be still active. Once the switch over has come about on just one occasion then the sequence of attention in the problem is changed, and this is what preserves the solution. There does not have to be a permanent change of emphasis at the switch point.

The insight phenomenon is not only possible on the special memory surface but is inevitable, since the actual sequence in which patterns are activated determines the outcome as much as the nature of the patterns themselves. Thus the special memory-surface is capable of both the gradual type of learning and also the sudden insight type.

The insight type of learning is extremely valuable because a certain pattern sequence, which has been built up that way because of chance encounters with information, can suddenly be restructured to make maximum use of that information. The other important point is that if insight is due to a change in the entry point into a sequence, then one can deliberately increase the possibility of insight solutions. This would be done by attention not to the problem itself but to the surroundings or antecedents of the problem, so that the entry point might be changed. It could also be done by deliberately starting attention at different points, or even by using random disrupting stimuli from outside. All this is dealt with later under lateral thinking.

HUMOUR AND INSIGHT

In humour there is a sudden switch over from one way of looking at things to another. This is exactly similar to the insight process. Both processes indicate the type of system that must be operating. Neither insight nor humour could occur in a system that proceeded in a linear fashion as does a computer. In a linear system the best possible state would always be the current one, and there would be no question of suddenly snapping over to an insight solution.

It is interesting to suppose that the pleasure of humour is related to the sudden pleasure of insight solutions. Indeed, when people are suddenly shown an insight solution to a problem they often burst out laughing. This pleasure may well be an essential part of the insight mechanism because the pleasure of solution enables the solution point to become the starting-point in the problem sequence, and in this way the solution is retained.

On the whole the insight mechanism is an extremely valuable one for information-processing, because it enables the maximum value to be obtained from information which has had to organize itself according to the time of arrival on the memory-surface. The insight mechanism compensates to some extent for this deficiency. Effective though insight may be, it is a haphazard and unreliable process.

The reality of the insight switch over from one way of looking at a situation to another is shown by an arrangement of ten coins in the form of a triangle, as on page 212. The triangle points to the top of the page and the problem is to get the triangle to point to the bottom of the page by moving only three coins.

There are several ways of doing this, but many people find it rather difficult, perhaps because they get confused by the number of different approaches that can be tried. On page 212 is shown what is probably the most elegant solution. Instead of being regarded as a triangle, the pattern is regarded as a rosette with three extra points. If each point is moved round to the next position the triangle is reversed. The interesting thing here is that once the solution has been seen and seen to be effective it becomes permanent at once.

In all these problem-solving situations one probably ought not to ignore the fact that there is a definite starting situation and a desired end situation, and that a solution does link the two up so creating one coherent pattern out of two separate ones. In itself this physical change on the memory-surface might account for the way in which in a problem situation a single occurrence leads to a permanent record, whereas on other occasions the basic pattern may only be changed by repetition. It may be a matter of the absence of competing pathways. Problem solutions which require the addition of some last bit of information that completes the circuit often give the impression of an insight solution.

FURTHER WAYS OF CHANGING THE BASIC PATTERN

When a particular pattern of thought-flow leads to some action, then the result of that action can lead to further activity on the special memory-surface. If you feel hungry you might pick an apple, and then the sight of the apple will suggest the use of a knife to peel it, and so on. It could of

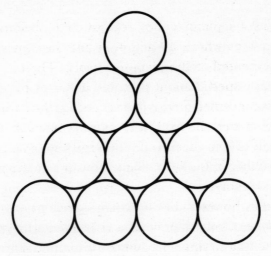

Fig. 80

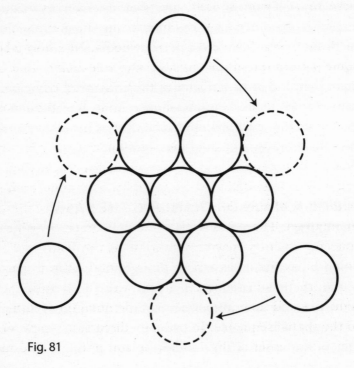

Fig. 81

course all be planned beforehand, but obviously there are situations where an action results in a new pattern being presented to the memory-surface. There is nothing particularly special about this, and as far as the memory-surface is concerned there is just a change in the environment. It cannot matter whether this change occurred on its own or as a result of some action. If as a result the basic pattern is changed, then this will be changed by one of the processes described before.

It might, however, be worth considering here a rather special type of behaviour which can facilitate change on the memory-surface. This behaviour is only a special example of any other action that changes the environment. The action here is that of writing, or notation, in the course of thinking.

The importance of the sequence in the natural flow of thought has been stressed repeatedly. Notation takes some pattern out of the sequence and freezes it in time by transferring it to paper. That pattern can then come back into the sequence at another time. Thus new sequences can be set up and the benefits of a change in sequence can be considerable. It is not, however, much use leaving the feature in notation form on a piece of paper, for then it will only be attended to when its natural turn comes round in the flow of attention. And that way the sequence will be maintained. There has to be some deliberate or artificial time for re-entry, paying attention to the feature. This could be as simple as arranging the notation in a spatial sequence that had nothing to do with the natural flow sequence and then just going over the notation according to the spatial sequence. In ordinary discussion a new idea may often be set off by another person putting back into your mind an idea out of its natural sequence. In argument this is exactly what one tries to do in order to change the other person's viewpoint.

CUMULATIVE EFFECT

All the methods described so far are ways in which the natural development of a pattern can be improved. Each special memory-surface has its own unique experience and from this develops its own established patterns. This unique experience can be so structured by education that the established patterns end up as being rather similar.

One can improve on the unique experience of a single memory-surface by pooling the experience of several, through communication. This ought to give more effective organization of the information available, because idiosyncrasies of experience would be ironed out. In practice this system does not work as well as it might. Very often the idea that results is not formed from common experience but from the unique experience of one individual, and is then accepted by the others. Also, pooling of information can just as firmly establish an erroneous pattern, if this arises from common experience; for instance, the idea that the sun goes round the world.

On the whole, communication probably does improve the established patterns by freeing the information available for self-organization from the chance nature of individual experience. For the same reason it might make difficult those new ideas that arise precisely from the chance nature of individual experience.

EFFORT AND CHANGE

One striking thing emerges from consideration of how the established patterns on the special memory-surface can come to be changed, and this follows directly from the way the surface is organized. On some occasions the slightest change at a sensitive point can lead to a huge over-all change. On other occasions no amount of effort at an insensitive point will lead to the slightest over-all change.

CHAPTER 24

LIMITATIONS OF THE SPECIAL MEMORY-SURFACE

The special memory-surface is a very effective device for processing information, but like all other effective devices it has its limitations. These limitations are inseparable from the advantages of the system since both arise from the same processes. If one is moving rapidly towards some point then there is an opposite point away from which one is moving just as rapidly. Precisely because the special memory-surface is excellent at some functions, it is rather poor at the opposite functions.

The limitations of the special memory-surface can take one of three forms:

1. Inability to carry out certain functions.
2. Actual errors.
3. Inefficient use of information available to it.

MOMENTUM

This fault is by no means peculiar to the special memory-surface but occurs in any system that uses 'trigger' communication. With time, fixed patterns are established on the memory-surface. When one fragment or several fragments of such patterns are encountered in the environment, then the rest of the pattern is supplied by the memory-surface. The fragment encountered merely serves to identify the pattern, just as a library number might identify a book. The memory-surface then reacts not to what is actually present but to its own pattern of what should be present. Sometimes this sort of reaction is inescapable, because there is only a fragment of pattern available. At other times the whole pattern is available but for the sake of speed it is more convenient for the memory-surface to use its established pattern. This system is immensely useful because it means that the reaction can be full and appropriate even if what is presented on the memory-surface is poor and incomplete. It also means that definite patterns can be established instead of a large variety of slight variations. The system is also useful because it allows reaction to take place before the event itself. Thus a doctor will treat the first symptoms of a disease when he elaborates the minor initial symptoms into a full-blown diagnosis. By such anticipatory treatment he actually avoids what is being reacted to.

Most of the time one is not reacting to what is present in the environment but only to established patterns which are triggered off by what is present. One follows the established pattern, but probably also keeps an eye on the environment picture in case the two patterns should get very far apart. The memory system is just guessing in terms of its accumulated experience.

Any system of this sort is open to guessing errors if something starts off as usual but then changes to something else. The momentum of the established pattern that is at first triggered off may lead to a reaction that is inappropriate for what really has happened.

Most people play tennis badly because they are too keen to hit the ball. They watch the early flight of the ball and then imagine the rest. They would play much better if they were to actually watch the ball right up to the last moment instead of hitting where they imagine the ball to be. The actual flight must always be more accurate than an imagined flight.

If spelling mistakes are made in the second half of words they are much less often noticed than if they are made in the first half. If the first few letters are sufficient to identify a word then the rest is imagined rather than read.

The momentum fault does not only apply to completion of a pattern but also to interpretation of a pattern, even when all the pieces are carefully examined. Here it is a matter of using elaborations that may always have to be used in interpretation. On page 219 is shown a picture of an impossible object. It is impossible because the way the lines are drawn lead on to a three-dimensional elaboration which has been established by experience; and in this particular case the elaboration is made to contradict itself.

The famous Ames distorting room is a room which appears to be perfectly ordinary and rectangular when viewed through a hole in the side wall. The odd thing is that a person standing at one end of the room appears to be very much larger than a person standing at the other end. In fact the room is not rectangular at all, but tapered. The eye assumes it to be rectangular because this is the established pattern for rooms. As a result of this assumption, a man who is really standing quite close is assumed to be far away, and is therefore seen as being a large man far away instead of a normal man close at hand.

Fig. 82

Exactly the same sort of illusion happened to me one day when I noticed a 'FOR SALE' sign hanging on a house which I took to be far down the street. Suddenly it became obvious that the notice was in fact hanging on a house that was much nearer. At once the notice visibly shrank in size. The striking effect of visual illusions due to incorrect elaboration may be due to the fact that there is no true picture with which to compare things as there usually is in other cases of mistaken elaboration.

A sequence of events can also give rise to the momentum error. It is an old schoolboy trick to ask someone to pronounce 'Mac-donald' when this is spelled out as 'M-a-c-d-o-n-a-l-d'. This is then followed with 'Macadam', 'Macbeth', 'Mackay' and finally 'Machinery'. There is a squeal of delight when machinery is pronounced as if it were a Scottish name. Another schoolboy trick is to ask someone how many pennies there are in a dozen. Immediately the answer is given, the person is asked how many halfpennies there are in a dozen. Often enough the answer is twenty-four (but the answer is actually twelve).

Stage magic relies almost wholly on the momentum error. The audience is led to make assumptions or elaborations that are perfectly reasonable, but do not in fact match what is being done in front of them.

The momentum fault is inescapable if the system is going to retain its speed of reaction by using fixed patterns and the 'trigger' type of communication with the environment. The errors are not in fact very frequent because the special memory-surface is so good at establishing patterns that are correct. It is not often that one goes wrong by taking things for granted. But when it does happen, it can be disastrous.

Some time ago when a series of new houses had been completed it was found that the ceilings, doors and windows all seemed to be rather low. They were. The explanation was that some saboteur had cut a few inches off the measuring stick which everyone took for granted as being correct.

The momentum error can be dangerous because at the time there is no way of telling that it is an error. Quite often one is not even aware that one is using an established pattern rather than reacting to the environment. If the discrepancy is pointed out or becomes obvious then one can examine the environment. But if it is not pointed out, or the environment is no longer there to examine, then the possibility of error is not even recognized.

Reacting to things as they should be, rather than as they are, is bad enough. Reacting to things as if they are going to turn out in a certain way, when in fact they are not, is probably worse. But both are small prices to pay for the general efficiency of the system. After all, elaboration is the basis of recognition, and without that the system would not function at all.

CHAPTER 25

MYTHS

The nature of the special memory-surface can give rise to myths, that is, patterns which exist on the special memory-surface but not necessarily anywhere else. This is both an advantage and a disadvantage of the surface.

The limited attention span of the special memory-surface divides up pictures which are presented to the surface. The complete picture is broken down into separate attention areas. Through the effect of short-term memory, these separate areas are usually re-combined as a sequence on the memory-surface to give a coherent pattern again. Thus the fragmentation is no more than a step in transmitting the complete picture to the surface, a way of changing space into time and then back into space again.

The division of the environment into attention areas is arbitrary. Sometimes these divisions may be natural ones that are evident in the environment; more often they are created by the memory-surface. This hardly matters if the division is a temporary one for the convenience of the memory-surface.

On page 224 is shown the d-line diagram of a complete picture which has been divided into four attention fragments. These are then reunited on the memory-surface and repeated emphasis establishes them as a coherent unit as shown. It may happen, however, that one of the created units, perhaps through connections with other things, becomes emphasized more than the other units. Through emphasis it becomes a separate entity on its own: it has become an arbitrary creation of the memory-surface. It would be quite easy to look at any object and divide it up into a top half and a bottom half. This would not matter if the two halves were reassembled as the complete pattern. It might even be a convenient method of description for objects such as dresses or football-league tables. But if the top half of everything was for some reason imbued with special significance 'because it was the half nearer heaven', while the bottom half was imbued with quite different qualities 'because it was earthly and basal', then instead of owing their allegiance to each other as parts of the same object the two halves would be pulled apart and would come to exist as separate entities.

This process is shown in d-line form on page 225. The top diagram shows the two halves reunited as a whole unit. The bottom diagram shows the two halves being pulled apart to form separate units with some other d-line complexes. This is a true creative division, since it exists only on the special memory-surface and not in the objects encountered. If both halves were equally emphasized then they might still persist as a unit made up of two halves with very different properties. If, however, only one half was emphasized then this would tend to take off on its own as a separate unit.

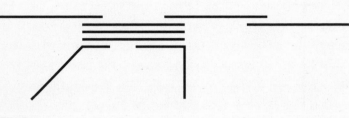

Fig. 83

Fig. 84

Descriptive labels become attached to the divisions created by the special memory-surface. It is rather difficult in visual terms to think of one side of the body as being a separate unit to the other side. But as soon as one attaches the labels 'right' and 'left' then these labels can separate in a way the physical body cannot. Each label can become the centre of a little complex of significance. Labels not only preserve the divisions of convenience made by the memory-surface but become little objects in their own right. This is why they are so very useful, for this results in a mobility which the original fragments could never have had. The words can be put together in groups or complexes that would have been most cumbersome without the use of words. And then the groups themselves get labels. By this time the actual objects which lay at the bottom of the hierarchy may be completely ignored.

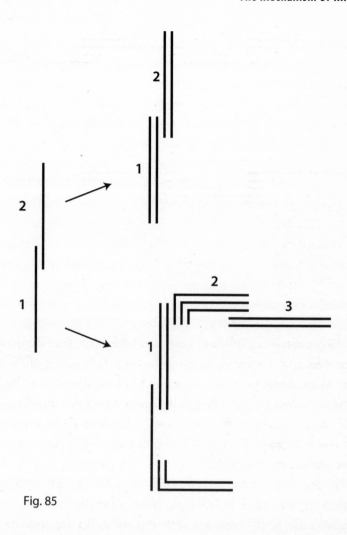

Fig. 85

The powerful combining property of short-term memory on the special memory-surface can combine fragments from quite separate objects to form a new object that only exists on the memory-surface: a centaur, a fairy or a fire-breathing dragon.

These creative and combining properties of the memory-surface result in an artificial world that is derived from the actual world but is not parallel to it. In this artificial world the information is organized with greater clarity and greater convenience. If no framework exists to do this, then one inevitably evolves. It may be necessary to create special systems of anthropomorphic gods to organize the information of the seasons, of the weather, of the behaviour of the crops. These organizing patterns which exist on the memory-surface are myths. Myths are more necessities than conveniences.

The myth arises as a way of connecting into a convenient coherent pattern the separate pieces of information that are derived from the environment. But once the myth is established it becomes a way of looking at the world. The world is seen through the myth and therefore tends to reinforce it. If you conceived the idea that mini-car drivers were dangerous and reckless then you would pay special attention to mini-car drivers and be quick to classify as dangerous any slight mistake in their driving. So the myth would be reinforced. From an information-processing point of view this system is very effective, because it magnifies slight differences and establishes firm patterns.

Myths tend to be self-perpetuating, since the accumulated information on the memory-surface provides the framework for processing incoming information. How then do myths change?

In the old style philosophical discussion the world was divided up into features, and then one played around with these features to see how they could be put together to make a sensible structure. Not surprisingly, one ended up with a structure which was implicit in the original choice of units of description. If you look at things through particular spectacles, then what you will see is not the thing itself, but the thing looked at through particular spectacles. If you look at the world through a transparent green sheet, then everything will appear green. No matter how hard you look at things through this sheet, that will only make them look greener. Nor is it any use looking at yourself to see if you are looking through a special coloured sheet. If you look at yourself in the mirror you would be completely unable to tell the colour of the sheet through which you were looking. The sheet would in fact appear greyish whether it was green or red or any other colour.

You would go through life looking through this green tinted sheet and believing that your view of the world was correct, even though other people told you that your view was in error. Then one day you would get into a car and drive off. At the first traffic lights you would be unable to see the red light through the green sheet and another car would smash into you. You would regret the accident and recover. Then it would happen again. At this point you might be ready to believe those who told you that your view of the world was mistaken and that you ought to get rid of the green sheet.

Escape from the convenient myths organized by the memory-surface comes about when these myths conflict with actual experience. Science is a way of specially organizing experience so that it can conflict with and show up the myths. In the process, new myths will be generated. A myth or hypothesis nearly always outlasts its usefulness and holds back a better interpretation of the available information but this is a minor limitation, a small price one has to pay for the usefulness of the myth system.

But there are myths which cannot be disrupted by experience. This can come about either because the content of the myth is not checkable by common experience or because the myth is so constructed as to turn what should disrupt it into support.

A paranoid, harbouring the myth of persecution, will point out the evidence for persecution in the very events that are offered to convince him that there is no persecution. If a particular myth leads to misery rather than happiness then it would seem that the myth would become disrupted. But if the myth explains that misery is really the best form of happiness in terms of penance, expiation, or even the Eastern idea of release from self-interest, then the myth is protected. If the myth goes further, and regards misery as an investment in future happiness, then the myth becomes self-perpetuating under all circumstances.

If something seems to be true then people will accept it; if it seems to be untrue then people will reject it. But rejection and truth can be made into the same thing by saying that what is true will be uncomfortable and hence rejected. This makes any explanation invulnerable and the myth involved self-supporting. If the myth offers love as an explanation for some phenomenon but it turns out to be hate, this does not damage the myth which explains that love and hate are really the same thing anyway. These are the sort of arguments that people use against psychoanalysis.

Extrasensory perception has proved a difficult subject to investigate. Experimenters are always offering up evidence of this phenomenon, but suspicious people who set out to check the results never seem to be able to reproduce the results of those who are in favour of the idea. The explanation suggested is that suspicious people are not in the right frame of mind to get results, that one must be confident and relaxed for extrasensory perception to get through. This makes the phenomenon insusceptible of critical investigation. It is rather like seeing ghosts. Only the sensitive people see ghosts, so you cannot prove that ghosts do not exist but only that you are not sensitive enough to see them.

It is quite easy to find self-protective situations. In my book, *The Use of Lateral Thinking,* I pointed out the rigidity of vertical thinking and the need for the flexibility of lateral thinking. But some vertical thinkers were so rigid that they could not even appreciate the need to be less rigid. In the present book many of the points are made in an easy manner and the intention is to stimulate the reader into realizing the full implications for himself. The danger is that a superficial reader who is unable to work out anything for himself might feel that things have been put down too simply. Because some myths are protected against destruction in the manner indicated above, it does not mean that they are false. If a man is shouting at you in a strange language that you do not understand, that does not mean that he must be talking nonsense. A myth can be like a self-consistent language. Once one accepts and understands the language, it makes sense. From outside it may not. The real point, however, is not whether the language is consistent but whether it is useful.

Since myths are by nature uncheckable, usefulness is a better criterion to apply to them than truth. The usefulness of a myth arises from its function as an organizing system for holding information together to provide a framework for easier acceptance of further information. The danger of a myth is its ability to exclude further information or better arrangement of information already available.

A woman went to a psychoanalyst who at one point asked her if as a child she had ever been afraid that she might be sucked down the plug-hole with the bathwater. She thought a while and then admitted that she had had such fears. It was explained to her that her basic trouble was insecurity and a fear of impending doom. For some weeks the woman felt much better. Then one day she met her mother and told her what had happened. Her mother roared with laughter and pointed out that there had been no plug-holes as they had only been able to afford tin baths. At once this destroyed the story and the useful effect it had had on the woman. The validity of the story as an organizing structure had been quite independent of its truth. It might also be said that a woman who believed she had had such fears would have been quite capable of having them, and hence the diagnosis was still valid.

Myths cannot be destroyed by direct attention since they are the organizing pattern on the memory-surface, and any attention to a pattern can only reinforce it. A myth can only be destroyed through inattention, which lets it atrophy so that a new organizing pattern can arise. Inattention or neglect usually follow when a myth has outlived its usefulness.

A dangerous myth may survive because it expressly forbids the circumstances which might contradict it. In Vietnam there is a myth that when children are ill they should not be given milk to drink as it causes diarrhoea. So the children are given only rice-water, which has no vitamins, and as a result they suffer severe vitamin deficiencies leading to blindness and even death. The myth is a self-perpetuating one since if children who have been kept off milk for some time are given milk they do get a temporary diarrhoea. This diarrhoea would pass off after a few days, but it is enough to reinforce this myth. This type of myth also indicates how impossible it is to suppose that natural phenomena will organize themselves into useful myths, and that useless myths will die out.

Myths are internal organizing frameworks for information. Such frameworks may increase the usefulness of available information by putting it together into a coherent structure that it would not otherwise have. But the arrangement of information contained in a myth may also be considerably worse than the best arrangement of available information.

CHAPTER 26

POLARIZATION

Every medical student believes himself to be suffering from almost all the diseases he reads about in his medical textbooks at the beginning of his training. Cancer, hole in the heart, diabetes, schizophrenia, syphilis and tuberculosis are all in turn suffered in the imagination. Everyone has vague symptoms which appear whenever they are attended to. As soon as the medical textbooks give definite names to symptoms and organize them as diseases then the vague symptoms are polarized to give complete diseases.

Words are drains which channel away in fixed patterns the meaning of any situation to which they are applied. The new situation dissolves into ready-made units or words. Nothing is left of it except flow through the well-worn word channels.

Words are mini-myths. They are for the convenience of the memory-surface in organizing the outside world in a more sensible manner than is apparent. The mechanical properties of the special memory-surface divide up presented pictures into attention areas. The walking-stick shown on page 233 is divided up into a curved handle, a sharp ferrule end and a middle shaft which joins the two. These are descriptive divisions which sometimes take off on their own to become units in their own right as described before. As creations of convenience, words provide these mini-myths that go on reinforcing themselves each time they are used. Once a particular way of dividing something up, or a unit, or an attention area, have become established then they drain off anything in the vicinity, just as a depression on the surface of either the jelly model or the polythene and pins model drained off water from nearby areas. This draining effect, and the tendency of established units to separate things, is what might be called polarization. The North Pole attracts

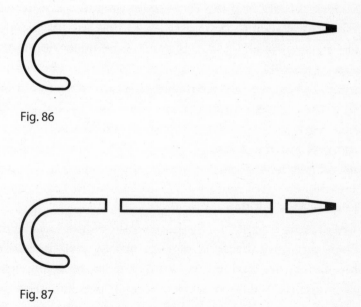

Fig. 86

Fig. 87

one end of the compass needle but rejects the other. A word will attract a particular piece of information and reject other pieces. Established units parcel up the information that is available to the memory-surface. The convenience of this procedure is obvious, for it has a selecting, discriminating and standardizing function.

Words are not only useful for making attention-fragments into things on their own, but also for creating things out of vague assemblies of other patterns. A group of painters start painting in ways which are different from the old ways. For a while there is some confusion and searching around, as the new style is manifestly different from the old one but rather difficult to describe. Then some art critic comes up with a name such as Dadaism, or Cubism, or Primitive. At once the whole thing clicks together and the different painters are seen to be exponents of that particular style. The name provides a unifying theme or polarizing point which makes for great convenience in talking about what is going on. It may also be damaging to the individuality of the painters, since the emphasis must fall on that part of their work which is related to the named style rather than that part which is distinct.

STATIC DIVISIONS

These are just divisions of convenience which enable attention to be directed to part of a thing at a time. The parts are treated as separate things which can then be worked upon. In physics, new particles are being discovered all the time. No sooner is it agreed that matter and energy can be explained in terms of a certain number of particles than someone discovers a new one. Many of the particles seem to be different states of the same particle. A different name is then given to each state because it makes for ease of description. It is as if one dropped a pebble to the ground and the pebble was given a different name when it was in your hand, when it was travelling through the air, when it hit the ground, and a final name as it lay on the ground. There must be a convenience in doing this, otherwise it would not be done. Yet even this division of convenience can have the disadvantage of rigidity in that it can keep apart things that are really the same.

For centuries it was convenient to consider matter and energy as being distinct. Then along came Einstein and showed that the two were really interchangeable: matter was a particular form of energy and the other way round. This idea is simple enough to accept for someone who has been brought up in this context, but other people would have difficulty in getting rid of the old and rigid separation of matter and energy.

As I grew up in a country which did not have many trees I never did learn the proper names of trees. To this day I look at trees as interesting and individual patterns without being able to put them together as a classification. I do not have to look at a tree through its label or through its standard group image. This may have some aesthetic advantages but it would have practical difficulties if I were a gardener or even if I wanted to describe a particular landscape to someone.

Perhaps the most striking example of polarization is the separation of the self from the surroundings. The convenience of this polarization is great. The polarization also suggests itself in terms of the separateness of the body and its mobility. Eastern philosophy regards this polarization as unnecessary and harmful: the troubles of man are seen to arise from the encouragement of this natural polarization. Great efforts are made to destroy the polarization. The final reward is to sink back from this individual polarization into a oneness with nature. Western philosophy takes exactly the opposite view and goes to great lengths to build up the self by means of emphasis on individuality and responsibility. Suffering and reward, penance and achievement, all tend to establish the individual self as a strong polarization and separate it from the background ever more distinctly.

MOBILE DIVISIONS

Static divisions simply chop things up into separate units of convenience. With mobile divisions, once the division has been made then the units actually move farther and farther apart. Static division is like cutting a piece of string. The fragments are separate but retain their same length and position. Mobile division is like cutting a piece of stretched elastic. The two ends spring apart. Static division is like breaking up a biscuit. The fragments retain the same shape and position. Mobile division is like dividing up a blob of quicksilver. The fragments separate and form themselves into tiny blobs on their own. Both processes occur very readily on the special memory-surface. If the unit remains on its own, then the division may be a static one. If the unit becomes drawn into some other complex, then the division will be a mobile one. The two are not always distinct. On page 237 is shown a pattern

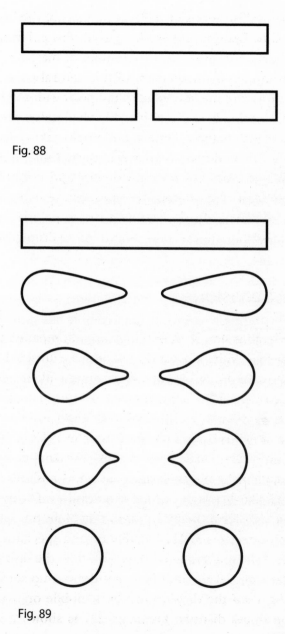

Fig. 88

Fig. 89

which is divided up in both ways. In the first instance the units remain where they are, in the second they retract away from each other.

A continuous process of change is divided at some convenient point. What comes before that division is called cause and what comes after is called effect. Then both cause and effect retract to become quite definite and distinct things on their own. They no longer appear to lie just each side of an arbitrary division.

People with slightly different views on some issue draw farther and farther apart. Finally they settle down as being politically opposed to such an extent that they do not agree on anything, and even make a virtue of disagreeing. They end up under such labels as Labour and Conservative, or Republican and Democrat. The differences may have been minor in the first place but polarization has pulled them apart. A politician is always pushed to the right or to the left. Whatever he says has to be polarized one way or the other. On account of the extremism of this outlook the term centre was created for those who could not be pushed either way with a clear conscience. But then the terms right of centre and left of centre arise and one is back to the old polarization again.

Another type of mobile division occurs when there is some fixed watershed. Just as rainfall flows down one side or the other of a sharp ridge, so a point of division may arise first and then categories develop on either side of it. This occurs with the jelly model when two depressions develop side by side. Another example is given by the corrugated surface onto which marbles were dropped. The ridges of the surface forced the marbles to move one way or the other.

With the first type of mobile division, once the cut was made the parts retracted naturally to become separate. With the second type there is some watershed which actually forces the units apart. The same effect is obtained with rigid boxes or pigeonholes.

Some time ago the avant-garde magazine *Oz* decided to experiment with its format and put out an issue in the form of a single folded sheet. The tax people pounced on this and said that it was no longer a magazine but a poster and as such would have to pay purchase tax. Yet the actual format was only one of several experimental formats that the publishers had in mind, and not all that different from an ordinary magazine. But it had crossed the watershed and was propelled as a result into the distant category called posters which contains things quite different from magazines.

Law, justice and practical administration depend entirely on this process of discrete pigeonholes. When reaction only follows an event then it can be flexible and fitting. Where reaction has to be laid down before the event even occurs, then it must rely on sharply divided categories which are firmly maintained.

Labels give rise to sharp categories. Anything that can sit under a label sits right under the centre of it. Anything else is shut out. Labels do not have to be words; signs or signals will do as well.

One day I was having lunch on the river-bank when a duck family waddled up to beg some food. There was a pompous drake, a dowdy female and five disenchanted ducklings. Presently another duck couple with a single offspring moved up. All at once the rather superfluous drake assumed his positive role. Lowering his head and rocking from side to side he charged at the intruders and drove them off. Yet when another species of bird descended nearby and competed very successfully for the food the drake paid no attention. It was not that the drake was naturally aggressive, it was just that he put the other drake into an objectionable category but the other bird he did not. The other drake had some visual label which set off the aggressive reaction.

It is usually assumed that aggression is a basic and uncontrollable instinct that must dominate animal behaviour. It is assumed that such basic drives override the intellectual functions, which are unable to control them. Yet the release of the basic instincts depends on the recognition of labels, and both this and the handing out of labels is often an intellectual function. The power of the basic instincts is like the powder in a gun. The effectiveness of a gun depends at least as much on when the trigger is pulled and where the gun is pointed as on the charge.

The power of a simple label change is often underestimated. A man about to leave his wife may be deterred by her tears and entreaties. He may be even further deterred if his friends refer to his plans as being 'ruthless'. Yet the situation can change completely if someone applies the label 'emotional blackmail' and suggests that he is the victim of this. At once the tears change from something that might be responded to into something that must be resisted at all costs. Yet this is just an intellectual change of label.

In the third type of mobile division, creation of a particular unit brings about the creation of an opposite unit. This could be called implied division. It is rather like finding one end of a stick and presuming that there must be another end somewhere. In this process one does not only imply that there is another end but also that the other end must be quite far away.

Any group that has a common enough interest for its members to think of themselves as 'we' at once implies the existence of another group which exists as 'they'. The division also implies a distance and separation of interests between the two groups. Once the groups have formed they tend to become more and more separate, like the polarization of political parties.

If one creates the idea of emotionalism one is not quite happy with the distinctness of the idea unless somehow it is set off against something else. One looks around for the other end of the stick and comes up with intellectualism. The two are then treated as opposite poles, qualities that are distinct and mutually exclusive. This implied division leads to the notion that an intellectual cannot be emotional, or that an emotional person cannot think. Yet in real life the passion of some intellectuals evidently exceeds the passion of many non-intellectuals.

The creation of the idea of free will at once implies the necessity for something called determinism which is opposite, distinct and separate. In fact something that has to be created in order to give distinctness to the idea of free will. Yet in truth the two things need not be opposite at all. To have free will it is enough to have the idea that one is exercising free will, whether or not this is an illusion. On the other hand the idea of free will is itself a determining factor. The two are not at all incompatible. Their incompatibility has only been created by an implied division procedure.

If one uses the idea of a memory-surface, then at once the idea of being able to read out from that surface is implied. One discards memory-surfaces from which read-out is impossible. Once again this implied division is false. Though memory-surfaces are usually accessible to read-out this is not essential. If the memory-surface is self-reading, if there is no one outside who has to read it, then read-out becomes unnecessary. In fact this is the case with the special memory-surface.

The creation of the idea of lateral thinking is a deliberate implied division to show up the deficiencies of vertical thinking. The idea is to rescue thinking from the strict polarization of sequential logic that has dominated it. By setting up an opposite pole one may counteract this tendency.

A particular danger that arises from the tendency to treat things in terms of opposite poles is that the poles become as far apart as possible. A stick is described in terms of its two ends, that is to say the very last bit of stick in either direction. Thus if there is a continuous gradation of feeling about some subject, this is never described in terms of the average feeling on either side of the midline but in terms of the absolute limits on each side. This is a natural tendency of the memory-surface, for unless two things are sufficiently far apart they will be treated as one thing. So any distinction at all is magnified into an absolute distinction. Exactly the same effect accounts for the process in which a partial description takes over as a total description. A politician is easily labelled as corrupt, even though only a small part of their behaviour justifies this description. But if this small part is the only part that is distinctive then it is taken as representative of the whole.

An interesting example of how implied division can be misleading occurred when I was discussing some medical treatment with a colleague who had had a classical education.

I mentioned that for a type of low blood-pressure the circulatory system could be made to cure itself by always keeping the patient tilted slightly upwards. I remarked that it would be nice if one could do the opposite for high blood-pressure, since this was so much more important an ailment. He agreed that it would be nice but alas one could not get flatter than flat.

For him, tilting upwards implied flat as the opposite and, as he said, one could not get flatter than flat. I was amazed, because to me the opposite of tilting upwards was tilting downwards, and flat was not something in itself but only a stage in the change from upwards to downwards tilt.

MECHANICS OF POLARIZATION

The two basic principles affecting polarization on the special memory-surface are movement and fixity. Movement can occur either when a pattern which lies athwart an old pattern becomes centred on the old pattern, or when a pattern gets bodily shifted to make it conform to an established one. Both processes are essentially the same, and both are shown diagrammatically on page 244. The other principle of the polarizing process is that established patterns are fixed and rigid.

On page 244 are shown two alternative types of categorization. The first type involves rigid pigeonhole boxes, and once something is put into one of these it stays there. The second type involves central posts, like flagposts, which merely proclaim a quality. Things are clustered around these posts but at different degrees of closeness. There is nothing

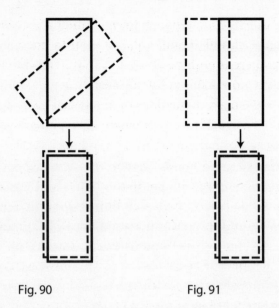

Fig. 90   Fig. 91

Fig. 92

Fig. 93

definite which separates them from another pole. Sometimes they may be classified under one label and sometimes under another; there is nothing absolute about it, it is just a matter of which is more likely at the moment.

One of the major limitations of the special memory-surface is that the categories are permanent. The patterns are established on a permanent basis. The memory-surface cannot comprehend that something may be one thing for a while and then the opposite for a while and then back again. There must be single labels, single definitions and permanent consistency. From a practical point of view this is convenient but can be limiting. To want to get rid of the fixed rigidity of the memory-surface does not mean advocating a wishy-washy formlessness but forms which may be just as definite at any one moment but not so permanent; something that can assume a variety of different shapes or change from one to another and back again. One would then become interested not in the static nature of things but in the range of their potential natures.

Connected with this major deficiency is the inability to entertain opposites at the same time. The idea of flexible-rigidity would be unacceptable, since this would straddle two opposite established patterns. Yet flexible-rigidity is perhaps an ideal state. Enough rigidity to give context, meaning and security. Enough flexibility to give change, improvement, adventure and hope. Another useful pair of opposites would be tough-humility; in a sense this is what early Christianity was about. A further pair of opposites is ordered-freedom, which simply implies enough order for people to be able to be free. Controlled-chaos means that by design chaos is allowed, in order that material may come together in unexpected ways which can then be harvested and developed further. All these pairs of opposites make sense, yet the tendency of the special memory-surface would be to keep them apart on the basis that what is flexible cannot be rigid, that humility cannot be tough, that order cannot produce freedom, that chaos cannot be controlled. In short that each pole was deliberately established as being distinct from the opposite pole.

CHAPTER 27

CONTINUITY

The whole functioning of the special memory-surface is based on continuity. The memory-surface processes incoming information by allowing accumulated information to interact with it. This is the only processing the surface is capable of. Each piece of information leaves its trace on the memory-surface, which becomes a record of all that has happened to it. Very gradually, the contours of the memory surface are formed. Established contours, established patterns, are there through continuity and repetition.

There are two basic ways of working things out on a computer. The first way is to put in some detailed formula for handling the information. The computer works through the formula and produces the answer. The formula provides a complete one-stage processing of the information. In the second method the computer carries out a simple operation that changes the information slightly, and then the operation is repeated on the changed information. This happens again and again until the final answer is reached. For instance, if the problem were to estimate the compound interest on a sum of money, the first method would use a formula to work out the final amount from the initial sum. The repetitive method would calculate the interest for the first year and then use this to calculate the interest for the second year, and so on. In this example the formula method would obviously be better, but in other cases the repetitive method would be much more accurate. If the problem were to calculate the flow-pattern around an object moving through the water, then the repetitive method would give the better answer. Since computers work so fast, the tediousness and time taken over the repetitive or iterative method does not matter.

The special memory-surface is a repetitive system. The changes are small and simple and each one builds on what has gone before. Continuity is the very essence of such a system. A gradual moulding of the contours can only take place if what has been moulded retains its form until the next stage in the moulding process. The special memory-surface always reacts in terms of what has happened in the past. No predictions at all can be made as to what might happen in the future, except by assuming that it must be exactly the same as the past. Things continue as they are until they are changed by something that has already happened. They cannot be changed by something that might be about to happen.

It is easy enough to balance one sugar cube on top of another. To go on doing it until a dozen or so are stacked is not so easy, a slight unevenness in the early stages will be magnified as the column gets taller. Finally the column topples over, and all because of the unevenness in the early stages.

Two travellers following slightly divergent pathways may not be far apart at the beginning, but as they proceed they will become farther and farther apart. The way established patterns get built up shows the same sort of continuity. When the slowly developing patterns diverge too far from reality, then novel things happen and the pattern tends to get changed.

It is customary in psychoanalytical theory to assume that behaviour in later life is largely determined by what has happened in the childhood years. The adult patterns are regarded as a continuous development of the childhood patterns. An aberration in childhood may continue to dominate the pattern, until in adult life the pattern is unsuitable, just as the column of sugar cubes was unstable on account of an irregularity in the early stages.

On the other hand, if the aberration leads to a pattern that is unusable then the ordinary process of adaptation will modify that pattern. So it is with information. Bit by bit information is built up in a continuous fashion, but when the gap between the established pattern and actual events is too large, then the pattern gets changed. The practical deduction from this is that big errors are better than small ones. With small errors the available information can be polarized to fit the errors. With big errors the gap is large enough for the information to be treated as new information which can disrupt and alter the established pattern.

Unless an established pattern is so wrong that it seriously interferes with the interaction between the memory-surface and the environment, it will not be corrected. What is just a different way of looking at things will persist. Wide differences in tastes and habits exist from country to country.

The French eat only a fraction as much ice-cream as do the English, and the English only a fraction as much as the Americans. This pattern tends to preserve itself, since the eating habits of the children are influenced by their parents, and also since a low consumption of ice-cream will not encourage a high expenditure on promoting ice-cream. The same sort of continuity accounts for the speaking of French in France and English in England. Changes can occur, as with the speaking of American English in the USA, but they are apt to be small and slow. It is not in the nature of the system to change itself suddenly.

The way information is built up on the memory-surface into established patterns is very much affected by the sequence in which the pieces of information arrive. Yet the best possible arrangement of this information should depend on the information itself, and not on the order in which it arrived. The time of arrival of the information adds a factor that should not be present in the final assembly of the information, if that final assembly is to be the best possible one.

The special memory-surface is a self-maximizing system, so at any one moment it will make the best arrangement of the information that is available at that moment. This pattern will tend to be preserved by continuity, even though further information is available which makes an alternative pattern possible.

On page 251 are shown two thin pieces of plastic which are given to someone with the instructions that they be arranged in a shape that can easily be described to someone who cannot see the pieces. The pieces always get arranged as shown to give a rectangle.

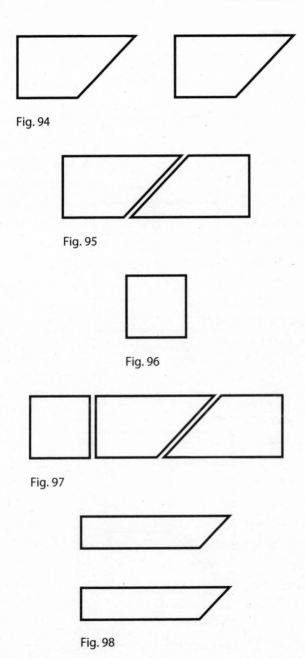

Fig. 94

Fig. 95

Fig. 96

Fig. 97

Fig. 98

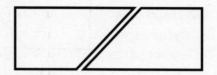

Fig. 99

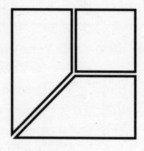

Fig. 100

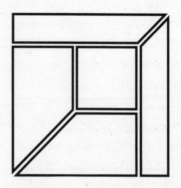

Fig. 101

This could be considered a self-maximization of the available information at this point. Then another piece is added as shown in Fig. 96 on page 251. The task is now to arrange the three pieces in a shape that is easy to describe. The result is usually another rectangle as shown on page 251. Then two further pieces are added as shown in Fig. 98. Very few people are able to complete the next stage.

The complete sequence is shown on page 252. The difficulty is that continuity and self-maximization make the second rectangle almost inevitable once the first one has been made. This is only natural. Yet considering the pieces as pieces, and disregarding the sequence in which they appeared, the square pattern is just as good an arrangement. From the square pattern the final arrangement is but a small step, but from the rectangle it is impossible. This example illustrates how the arrangement of information may make the best possible sense at the time and yet provide a block to further development. This is exactly the nature of the system that is operating on the special memory-surface.

The final arrangement of the five plastic pieces need not have taken the previous patterns into account at all. It could have been done by a pure arrangement of the pieces to give the best result. Unfortunately, the sequence of arrival of the pieces and the intermediate patterns do not allow such pure arrangement of information on the special memory-surface.

Because of the importance of the time of arrival of information, the current arrangement of information on the special memory-surface must usually be less than the best possible pure arrangement. At each intermediate stage the arrangement may have been right, but this does not ensure that the final arrangement is right, or even that it can ever be right, given these intermediate patterns. The only mechanism whereby this inherent limitation of the information-processing on the special memory-surface can be put right is insight. This is only a partial compensation, but even so the effect may be very striking. This insight mechanism has been discussed in Chapter 23.

CHAPTER 28

BIAS

So far the disadvantages of the pure, selfless, memory-surface have been considered. The next step is to consider how the selfish aspects of the body using the special memory-surface come to affect the information-handling on the surface. There may be needs such as hunger, thirst or sex. There may be reactions such as fear or anger. These are the things that are usually examined under the headings of emotion, mood, motivation, drive. Lumped all together, these are the things that produce internal patterns on the memory-surface. By internal pattern is simply meant some effect on the memory-surface that is over and above the pattern left by information coming from the environment.

In functional terms the only important point about these internal patterns is that they dominate the memory-surface. Whenever an internal pattern is activated then the active area on the memory-surface tends to include that pattern.

Normally the dominant area on the memory-surface is the one with the lowest threshold at the moment, and this is determined by what is being presented to the surface, what has been happening on the surface just before, and the degree of establishment of the various patterns on the surface. These are all pure information factors. The internal patterns provide an emphasis that is independent of these factors. A ball rolled along the ground will change direction according to the contours of the ground. But if, as in bowls, a bit of lead is fixed inside the ball to give a bias, then the direction of the ball will be dominated by this internal bias (though not to the complete exclusion of the effect of the contours of the ground). The bias provides an independent emphasis. It is in this sense that the internal factors can be lumped together as bias. The point to consider is how this bias affects the information-handling of the special memory-surface.

In practical terms the bias fluctuates over a period of time. When a particular bias is active then the established patterns which are emphasized by it become temporarily dominant over others, but this effect is not permanent. In pure information terms this variable bias can be extremely useful, for it means that there can be a change in the sequence of flow through established patterns if the bias changes. Such change is the basis of learning and insight. The same variability is also the basis of creativity.

In evolution there is a change process followed by a selection process. The natural development of patterns on the memory-surface is a process of gradual change. The bias process provides the selection. Those patterns which are particularly useful become emphasized temporarily and this leads to such frequent use that they become more established than the others. This selection process can make up for many of the limitations of the memory-surface, especially the continuity which might otherwise produce patterns that were widely divergent from reality and not much practical use.

Variability and selection are the useful aspects of the bias system. Bias can also interfere in a less useful way with information-processing on the memory-surface.

Since the direction of attention is merely the reflection of how the area of activation wanders over the memory-surface, bias plays a large part in directing attention. If one is hungry and driving through the streets, one is apt to notice cafés and restaurants more than anything else. This direction of attention has a certain usefulness, but it may mean that more useful information is ignored. In the example given, the ignored information might be a signpost or a no-entry sign. The ignored information may have been useful in itself, or dull in itself but useful when added to information already collected.

Even if the bias process provides useful selection at the time, this selection may come to be a disadvantage later. The businessman who hires an employee because they seem confident and friendly at interview, may discover that they are actually bad at their job.

There are instances in which the internal bias does not fluctuate as it ought, but is more permanent. For instance, if this happened with fear then the persistence of that bias would lead to the selection of those aspects of things which were frightening. Other people would be seen as attackers, motor vehicles as liable to run one over, dogs as vicious. In exaggerated form such a person would be unable to step outside his door. Even in a mild form the effect of this sort of bias on information-processing must be considerable.

Whenever the bias is particularly strong then the most directly relevant patterns become completely dominant over all others. In a panic situation fear is so strong that emphasis of the most directly relevant action, such as rushing to the obvious exit of a burning cinema, leads to the eclipsing of less direct but more useful patterns of action, such as looking for other exits. This is an extreme case, but the same effect is to be found in other situations. If a chicken is separated from food by a short length of wire netting then it will try to get directly at the food rather than move away from the food to get round the netting. A boy may drop out of school because he wants to earn and enjoy money quickly. The indirect approach through staying on longer at school in order to get a better job has less appeal. In practice this emphasis of the direct approach is rarely a disadvantage because often the direct approach is best, and when it is blocked then other approaches can be tried, just as a dog, unlike the chicken, would eventually walk round the wire fence. The major deficiency is that the direct approach may lead to a solution that is adequate enough to satisfy but much less effective than another solution. Beating someone over the head may be an adequate temporary solution to a troublesome problem but not necessarily the best possible solution.

In information terms, bias emphasizes the established patterns that have been most relevant in the past and may ignore the better arrangement of patterns that may be available on pure information grounds. Ultimately it is the bias system which alone can decide whether information is useful or not. But the bias system may actually be a disadvantage in the processing of information. Pure information-processing can sometimes produce a more useful result – as judged by the bias system – than if bias had influenced the information processing itself. It is not a matter of preferring the head to the heart, for ultimately the heart must be more important. But it may be necessary to realize that the head may be able to do more for the heart than the heart can for itself.

Perhaps the most important effect of the bias system is to be found when the bias is not particularly strong, not even strong enough to be recognized. In such cases the emphasis provided by the bias may be strong enough to divert thought-flow into a different path from the one it would otherwise have done, and yet it seems that the path is selected purely on an information basis. On page 260 is a d-line diagram showing the flow path in the absence of bias and then in the presence of bias, which is indicated by a wavy line. If you start off by disliking something then you can always find reasons to support that dislike. But your dislike appears to be based on the reasons.

The advantage of the bias system is that it provides an emphasis which is independent of the emphasis provided by the self-organization of the information coming in to the memory-surface. The disadvantage of the bias system is exactly the same.

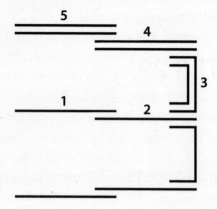

Fig. 102

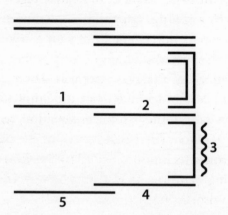

Fig. 103

CHAPTER 29

SUMMARY OF FAULTS

The errors, faults and limitations of information-processing on the special memory-surface are inescapable because they follow directly from the nature of the organization of the surface. The faults cannot be eliminated without also doing away with the tremendous advantages of this type of surface. Nor can the faults be eliminated by deliberate avoidance, since the system is a passive one. Nor is the recognition of the faults as they occur possible, because this implies an alternative pattern for comparison.

The only possible form of compensation for the faults is an awareness that they are inevitable, followed wherever possible by techniques of using the surface that minimize the faults. Such techniques are then fed into the surface as organizing patterns that can passively influence the information-processing.

Since the errors arise from the mechanical structure of the system they are strictly definable and predictable. Individual errors are not necessarily predictable, though they may be. But the general types of error are predictable.

The types of error may be summarized as follows. There is the establishing of definite units and patterns that become very rigid, so that in time these units and patterns tend to alter information rather than be altered by it. Organizing patterns become self-perpetuating as myths. The adequacy of all these patterns is impaired by the important part played by the time sequence of arrival of information. Finally there is an internal bias which operates in so blurred a fashion as to lead to distortion.

The self-correcting tendencies of the system are not sufficient to compensate for the deficiencies. The bias system acts as a useful selective process but a clumsy one. Insight can compensate for errors due to time of arrival of information, but it is haphazard and infrequent. Communication and pooling of experiences can eliminate errors, but can also magnify them.

Apart from the actual faults or errors there are inherent limitations in the system. The system is one that creates order out of chaos but imposes an old order rather than becomes aware of a new one. Recognition of a new order must inevitably lag behind the availability of such a new order in terms of information.

Perhaps the functional characteristics of the system can be summed up in a single phenomenon. This is the finding of an obvious solution to a problem that was very difficult. Only after the solution has been found is it seen to be obvious. Such behaviour is characteristic of a special type of information-processing.

CHAPTER 30

THINKING

Thinking is the flow of activity from area to area on the special memory-surface. The flow is entirely passive and follows the contours of the surface. There is no question of an outside agency directing where it should go. The sequence of activated areas constitutes the flow of thought. The flow may be continuous, that is from one area to an adjacent one, or activity may die out in one area to start up in another unconnected area. Where there is a pause there may be an image; where there is no pause there may be no image. Nevertheless the flow itself may be continuous whether the images follow one another or are intermittent. Although the flow is entirely passive, certain artificial organizing patterns which affect the direction of flow can become established on the surface. Such patterns have usually been fed onto the surface deliberately.

Four different types of thinking can be recognized. The basic nature of all these is still the passive flow of activity over the memory-surface, but in each case the artificial organizing patterns are different.

NATURAL THINKING

This could also be called raw, simple or even primitive thinking. The basic contours of the surface determine which way the flow goes, and there are no added artificial patterns to interfere with this. Flow is determined by the natural behaviour of the surface and as a result it has certain definite characteristics.

REPETITION

With natural thinking, if something is said three times then it is more right than something said only once. Repetition does give dominance and natural flow simply follows dominance. Natural thinking is also susceptible of perceptual dominance. A bright colour makes something more important than things with dull colours. A large man or a noisy person does become the most important person in the room.

Another characteristic of natural thinking is that it tends to be completely dominated by bias if there is an internal need operating. The patterns selected are the ones most connected with these needs and of these patterns the most directly related ones are more likely to be used than any other patterns. Thirst brings to mind a glass of beer and not the mechanism of drinking.

Another feature of natural thinking is the complete lack of proportion. If one Irishman happens to get drunk and becomes a nuisance then natural thinking reaches the conclusion that all Irishmen are always drunk. If some students rebel then all students are rebellious. With natural thinking emphasis is all that matters. One very drunk Irishman may give as much emphasis as a number of mildly drunk Irishmen. The fact that most Irishmen are not drunk cannot cancel the emphasis, because once the pattern is established it cannot be erased, only altered. And in natural thinking there is no way of altering a pattern since thought-flow just follows the emphasis.

The lack of proportion in natural thinking in some ways resembles the content of newspapers. The odd, the unusual, the emotional all get as much emphasis as ordinary events, or more, even though the latter are much more important in real-life terms. Labels and categories are much used in natural thinking since they provide quick interpretation and firm direction of flow. There is little vagueness or indecision in natural thinking, since even a slight degree of dominance in one area is sufficient to attract the flow.

The lack of proportion particularly applies to the recognition of alternatives. Because of the nature of the special memory-surface one pattern gets chosen to the complete exclusion of an alternative pattern, even if the other pattern was a very likely alternative. Since there is no hesitation with natural thinking, alternatives are never considered.

In general, natural thinking proceeds from image to image as directed by emphasis or bias. Classifications, names and labels mean more than actual statistical probabilities.

Natural thinking tends to move from one cliché to another. These clichés are the well-used patterns that have become established as units. Such units get larger and larger. Once the flow of thought has reached such a unit then it will follow the cliché pattern, completely ignoring variations, modifying factors or side-turnings. Natural thinking makes use of absolutes and extremes, since these patterns become more easily established than intermediate ones. Abstraction is rare in natural thinking because the momentum of established cliché patterns makes unlikely the use of only part of them. Natural thinking tends to use concrete imagery and personal experience rather than patterns that are second-hand and remote. With natural thinking the established cliché patterns are the important thing and the connecting links are trivial.

In some ways dream thinking is a caricature of natural thinking. With natural thinking, however, the flow sequence does reflect the natural order since this is what has established the contours of the memory-surface. With dream thinking there seems to be less of a sequence than the spontaneous activation of separate areas on the memory-surface. This spontaneous activation then becomes loosely linked together into some pattern through the flow that follows each spontaneous activation. With dream thinking the items come first and then the sequence second. With natural thinking the sequence comes first and the items second. But in both types the items or cliché patterns are more important than the connecting material.

In dream thinking it may be that the areas of activation are selected for their relevance or connection to an operating internal pattern, such as fear. This determines the roll call of items. With natural thinking the items follow on from one another in a natural order even though the emphasis may be unnatural.

In short, natural thinking is the natural way the memory-surface behaves. The flow sequence follows the contours of the surface. The thought-flow is immediate, direct and basically adequate. But it is also liable to very considerable error.

CHAPTER 31

LOGICAL THINKING

Natural thinking is very fluent. This very fluency is the source of its errors, for fluency means following emphasis of patterns however that emphasis might have come about. Logical thinking is an improvement on natural thinking because it trims the exuberance of natural thinking. Logical thinking is a deliberate attempt to restrain the excesses of natural thinking. This restraint is effected by selectively blocking natural flow pathways.

Logic is the management of NO.

Natural thinking tends to follow emphasized pathways, but when these pathways are blocked with a NO then the flow has to pursue other paths. This effect is shown diagrammatically on page 268. Most logical processes can be reduced to identity and non-identity. But if there is a sensitive mechanism for recognizing non-identity then nothing needs be done about discovering identity, as it will sort itself out. Logical thinking uses the flow of natural thinking but controls it by means of a sensitive mechanism for recognizing and labelling non-identity.

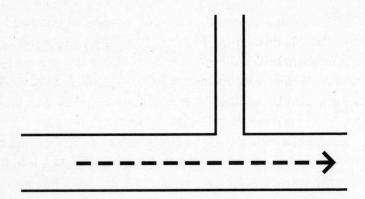

Fig. 104

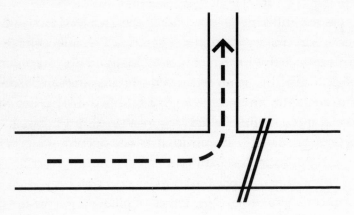

Fig. 105

There are two parts to logical control. The first part is the provision of a convenient device for labelling non-identity. This is NO, and all the various types of negative that come under that broad heading. The second part is training in the use of the device in order to develop a heightened sensitivity for recognizing those situations which demand the NO label.

Non-identity is but another term for mistake, or mis-match, or detectable difference. The use of NO implies recognition of a mis-match. For there to be a mis-match there must be two conflicting patterns on the memory-surface. How does NO come to be applied to one of these patterns, and how does it succeed in blocking that particular pattern?

It would be easy if there were some outside agency which simply recognized the mis-match and put a NO label onto it. But there is no outside agency, because the special memory-surface is a passive self-organizing system. This means that the NO label can only become attached as the result of some phenomenon on the memory-surface itself. A mis-match could provide a sufficient phenomenon if some physical state of the surface always accompanied a mis-match. A mis-match is a pattern of activation which tends to try and develop in two directions at the same time. This unstable state could well give rise to an internal pattern such as fear or tension. NO would then be the symbolic form of this distress. The symbolic form, like the distress itself, would become connected with the unstable pattern.

It does happen that a mis-match on the visual level gives rise to discomfort approaching nausea. If something is seen to be different from what is expected then there is such distress. The design of a national flag carried out in a different colour can give rise to the same effect. Monkeys become very distressed if a well-known keeper distorts his features by wearing a mask. The nausea of sea-sickness may have something to do with this mis-match effect, and aesthetic pleasure with its absence.

With training, this vague feeling of distress could be conveniently crystallized in the use of NO. NO would then act as emotional reaction. The more clearly NO was established as an emotional reaction during education, the more effective it might be later on. It would also be possible to predict that people who were incapable of the appropriate emotional reaction would be incapable of logical thinking. Quite possibly this could apply to some types of psychopaths.

In this view, NO would be as much a reaction to a general type of phenomenon on the memory-surface as humour or laughter is.

The NO reaction signals that the development of a pattern is not in accord with the already established pattern.

The question of how the NO label comes to have any effect is separate from that of how it comes to be applied in the first place. As another pattern on the memory-surface, the NO pattern, when attached to any other pattern, might divert the thought flow into a dead end so that the sequence would be blocked. This effect is shown in d-line form on page 271 where one of two alternative lines of flow is blocked by the attachment of NO. More important than this blocking by diversion might be the emotional content of NO as a fear or avoidance situation. NO would be a neat device for attaching an avoidance reaction to any particular pattern. Reduced to a formalized routine, this avoidance reaction would be of the same type as that elicited by fire after it had been found that fire hurt.

The interesting point about the management of NO is that on the special memory-surface it would derive its usefulness from its emotional content. The more emotion that was infused into the NO label by upbringing, the more powerful would be its use and its effect. Far from being an intellectual effect, logical thinking would be a basically emotional one, though a rather special type of emotion.

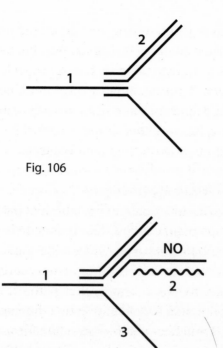

Fig. 106

Fig. 107

Since logical thinking is something added to control and make the most efficient use of natural thinking, the memory-surface would have to be trained in its use by an outside source. This training would consist in the development of an acute sensitivity to the mis-match reaction so that NO could be applied at an early stage. This would be the same as developing the aesthetic or humour reaction to a fine sensitivity. As part of the training the emotional content of the NO symbol might also be increased by punishment. Finally, the training in logical thinking would include the development of certain special ways of handling information, certain fixed patterns. Such fixed patterns are discussed in the next chapter. Their purpose in logical thinking would be to arrange the information so that the NO reaction could occur in a more blatant form.

The effect of logical thinking is like that obtained by a farmer who directs the water to his fields by careful blocking up of some irrigation channels, in order to get the water to flow through the others. Logical thinking is a great improvement on natural thinking, but it still has many limitations in terms of information-processing.

The too-early and too-easy attachment of the NO label can block pathways which might have been useful after all. This occurred with the hole in the postcard problem, where many people attached the NO label to the spiral pattern and so abandoned what was a road to the solution. Once the NO label has been attached then it is very difficult to reverse it should more information become available which makes it invalid. Once a NO label has been attached it is impossible to proceed along that pathway, yet there are occasions when it is necessary to pass through an incorrect area in order to get to a point beyond, from which the correct pathway is visible. Logical thinking trims and refines the natural thinking flow and allows seldom-used patterns to be used. But the actual patterns used are used in their established way. Logical thinking can never lead to that alteration of sequence that leads to the 'insight' rearrangement of information. The units used by logical thinking are still the same as the units used by natural thinking. Logical thinking may find out the best way of putting together A, B and C but it will not discover that A, B and C are inappropriate units anyway.

In spite of these limitations, logical thinking is obviously a tremendous improvement on natural thinking and is immensely effective. In terms of education, the same effect could probably be obtained without the use of the NO device to block pathways, by simple emphasis of the correct pathways so that these came to be used in their own right and not on account of the blocking of others. This would achieve the same effect but it would only provide fixed patterns, and would not give such a flexible tool for dealing with future situations.

CHAPTER 32

MATHEMATICAL THINKING

Tiny squiggly patterns in black on a white surface would seem to have little to do with the taste or texture of a sponge cake. Flour, eggs and butter would seem to have more to do with the cake, but even so they seem far removed from the finished cake. Yet the squiggly patterns in black on a white surface may be responsible for changing the flour, eggs and butter into the cake. The cake-making recipe is a written formula. The pattern set out in this formula is applied to the raw ingredients, and the result is a cake.

Mathematical thinking involves the use of such ready-made recipes. The recipes are not as specific as the cake-making ones but are general tricks and techniques for handling relationships. Some of the tricks and techniques are set out as detailed instructions, but it is more convenient to have general rules that can be applied in different combinations than to set out all the possible techniques. Mathematics is a game played with symbols and rules. The rules constitute a special universe in which things happen according to these rules. Anything enters this universe by being translated into a symbol. The symbol is processed according to the rules of the universe and then translated back at the end.

The rules and techniques of mathematics are worked out in advance, just as one might design and build a washing machine and then feed into it all sorts of laundry. Unlike what happens on the special memory-surface, the processing is not carried out by the information itself but arranged before the information ever arrives. Rather than let the information cut its own channels, these are dug beforehand and then the information has to follow these pre-set channels.

These pre-set channels are sometimes called algorithms. An algorithm is any fixed pattern which is not derived from presented information but serves to control and sort out that information. Algorithms may be mathematical techniques, but they may also be word patterns or any other type of pre-set pattern.

The Paul Jones was an algorithm which was often used at embarrassed dances when no one knew anyone else. The men linked hands to form a circle which revolved around a similar circle of women going in the opposite direction; when the music stopped the men were supposed to dance with the women in front of them. The whole procedure was an algorithm designed to process people into pairs.

Through their structure proteins can link up with one another, but the process would be rather haphazard. In order to ensure that the proteins link up in the right way, and so make heredity an accurate reproducing system, some better method is required than haphazard linkage. As on page 277, DNA provides a backbone rather like a hat-rack on which the proteins come to be hung. Each of the hooks is different and will only hold on to one type of protein.

The protein is also held in such a way that it can easily link up with its neighbour. In this way the proteins link up with each other and then fall away as a complete unit. The DNA provides a pre-set processing system which allows the information to link up in the most appropriate way. Mathematical techniques function in the same way.

Notation itself is a form of algorithm. Once a process has been translated into a notation model then the functioning of this model will constitute an algorithm for dealing with the process. When the change in velocity of a falling stone is changed into a graph line on a piece of paper, then one studies the possible behaviour of such a graph line and from this can predict all sorts of things about the falling stone. Notation creates its own universe, and a good notation can provide much information about relationships that can then be applied to quite other relationships.

In the universe of mathematics, information behaves according to the rules of that universe and not according to the rules of the special memory-surface. In this way most of the faults and limitations of the information-processing on the special memory-surface can be avoided. The result of this is an immensely effective method of information-processing that is responsible for technological progress. Even so, there are still limitations. The mathematical systems are themselves devised by creative rather than analytical methods. The systems themselves evolve and change in the same way as does any established pattern on the special memory-surface. New insight leads to great leaps forward in mathematical ideas, as with Descartes and his co-ordinate geometry, Newton and Leibniz with the calculus and Euler with topology. The great usefulness of Euclidean geometry was further improved by

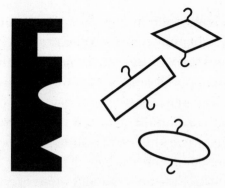

Fig. 108

Fig. 109

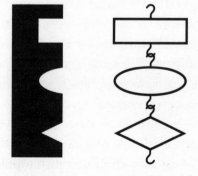

Fig. 110

the development of different geometries by Riemann and Lobachevsky. Doubtless there are many more ideas still to come, and they will have to come about through the workings of the special memory-surface which is so limited in its insight and creativity.

Before mathematical thinking can be used there is a preliminary stage in which the information has to be sorted out and then translated into symbols. This preliminary stage, which depends on the ordinary information-processing of the special memory-surface, involves the choice of units and the choice of a particular way of looking at things. Games theory is a powerful technique for dealing with the conflicting possibilities of a competitive situation. If one applies this theory to the story of *Othello* it is possible to end up with the odd conclusion that Desdemona ought to have deceived Othello and he ought to have murdered her. This represents the best play of each of them in this game. There is nothing wrong with games theory, but the outcome depends on what values are assigned to such things as ridicule, honour and loss of life. It is what is put into the technique that makes nonsense of the outcome. In the computer world there is an expression GIGO which means 'garbage in, garbage out'. Unfortunately the choice of what is put into the mathematical system is not itself determined by mathematical thinking but by the ordinary information-processing of the special memory-surface. Nor is the choice of mathematical techniques itself a mathematical technique.

There is the well-known problem of two cyclists who start thirty miles apart and cycle towards each other at fifteen miles an hour. A bee which flies at fifty miles an hour starts off from the nose of one of them, flies to the nose of the other, and then returns. If the bee shuttles back and forth in this manner until the cyclists meet, how many miles has the bee actually covered? It is assumed that the bee's pauses on the noses do not take any time at all.

This problem was apparently given to one of the greatest mathematicians of the century, who thought for a while and then realized that it could be solved by using a rather tricky mathematical technique for dealing with a diminishing series. He took some time to work this all out in his head and then gave the right answer. Many schoolboys, however, solve the problem in a much simpler way. They reckon that the cyclists will take an hour to meet and since the bee is travelling at fifty miles an hour it must have flown fifty miles. This elegant solution follows a shift in attention from the distance travelled to the time taken. One must suppose that because the mathematician was capable of working it out the hard way he never got as far as considering the easy way.

If there are one hundred and eleven entrants in a tennis tournament how many matches must there be? If this problem is given to most people they will at once start thinking in terms of those branching patterns that adorn notice-boards at tennis clubs. They start off by dividing the one hundred and eleven into fifty-five and one bye and then proceed. Or else they think in terms of powers of two. The neatest approach is to consider that there must be one winner and everyone else must lose and that means one hundred and ten matches each of which provides one loser.

Yet another problem of this type involves the breaking up into separate pieces of a bar of chocolate eight pieces long by four wide. If you cannot double up the pieces what is the smallest number of breaks necessary to separate each piece? Most people draw a diagram and then lines dividing up the diagram. The neatest solution is to consider that at each break there is one more piece than there was before that break, so for thirty-two pieces there cannot be less than thirty-one breaks.

These are all simple problems. The point they make is that the availability of a sound technique for solving a problem does not exclude the possibility of a better technique or the choice of a better approach. Neither choice of approach nor choice of technique is itself mathematically determined.

The above limitations of mathematical thinking, and in particular the difficulty of defining the initial units, may explain why it has not proved so useful in its application to people as it has to things.

CHAPTER 33

LATERAL THINKING

The purpose of lateral thinking is to counteract both the errors and the limitations of the special memory-surface. The errors may lead to incorrect use of information. The limitations may prevent the best use of information that is already available. Natural thinking has all the errors of the special memory-surface. Logical thinking is used to avoid the errors of natural thinking, but it is limited in that it cannot generate new ideas that make the best use of information already available. Mathematical thinking avoids the errors of natural thinking by setting up an information-processing system that is distinct from the memory-surface. The limitation of mathematical thinking is that it is only a second-stage system which is used to make the most of what has been chosen by the memory-surface in the first stage. None of these three types of thinking can get completely beyond the limitations of the memory-surface, though two of them can reduce the actual errors to a considerable extent.

A problem is simply the difference between what one has

and what one wants. Since a problem has a starting-point and an end point, then the change from one to the other by means of thinking is a direct indication of the usefulness of that thinking.

There are three basic types of problem:

1. Problems that require the processing of available information or the collection of more information.
2. The problem of no problem. Where the acceptance of an adequate state of affairs precludes consideration of a change to a better state.
3. Problems that are solved by a re-structuring of the information that has already been processed into a pattern.

The first type of problem can be tackled with logical thinking, or mathematical thinking, or the collecting of more information. The other two types of problem require lateral thinking.

Most of the time the established patterns on the special memory-surface are improved only by information which comes in from outside. It is a matter of addition or gradual modification. Lateral thinking is more concerned with making the best possible use of the information that is already available on the surface than with new information. Lateral thinking is concerned with compensating for the deficiencies of the special memory-surface as an information-processing device. Lateral thinking has to do with rearranging available information so that it is snapped out of the established pattern and forms a new and better pattern. This rearrangement has the same effect as insight. The established patterns which determine the flow of thought can be changed by lateral thinking, as can the established patterns which control how things are looked at.

The memory-surface itself, natural thinking, logical thinking and mathematical thinking are all selective processes. The memory-surface selects what it will pay attention to. Natural thinking selects a pathway according to emphasis. Logical thinking blocks pathways according to the mismatch reaction. Mathematical thinking uses the rules of the game to select possible changes. The only generative process involved is the chance arrangement of information in the environment.

A baby crying is a generative situation. The baby just makes a noise and then things happen. From all the things that happen, the baby accepts the ones that are useful to itself. Lateral thinking is a generative process. Instead of waiting for the environment to change established patterns, these are deliberately disrupted in various ways so that the information can come together in new ways. If any of these new ways are useful then they can be selected out by any of the selecting processes.

In the early days of photography, the photographer used to go to a great deal of trouble to arrange the background, the lighting, the pose, the smile, and then when everything was just right he took the photograph. Nowadays the photographer just takes dozens of pictures from different angles with different expressions and different lightings. Then he looks at all the pictures and picks out the ones that look best. In the first case the selection is done before the photograph is taken, in the second case it is done after the photographs have been taken. The first method will only produce what is known beforehand and planned. But the second method may produce something new that was totally unexpected and could never have been planned.

With the other types of thinking you know what you are looking for. With lateral thinking you may not know what you are looking for until after you have found it. Lateral thinking is like the second method of taking photographs, and the other sorts of thinking are like the first method. For convenience these other sorts can be included under the heading of vertical thinking, which is the sequential development of a particular pattern – like digging the same hole deeper. With vertical thinking one moves only if there is a direction in which to move. With lateral thinking one moves in order to generate a direction.

The generative effect of lateral thinking is exerted in two ways. The first way is to counteract, restrain, or delay the fierce selective processes of the memory-surface itself. It is also necessary to counteract the selective processes that have been artificially developed, such as logical thinking with its heightened sensitivity to a mis-match. The second way is to bring about deliberate arrangements and juxtapositions of information that might never otherwise have occurred. The aim of both these processes is to allow information to arrange itself in new and better patterns, as happens in insight.

The nature of lateral thinking may be illustrated by outlining a few specific points of difference from vertical thinking.

ALTERNATIVES

The special memory-surface is a self-maximizing system. The tendency of such a system is to select the most obvious approach, provided this is adequate. In an experiment a group of children were each given two small wooden boards. There was a hole in the end of each board, and the children were also given a piece of string. The task was to cross the room as if it were a river by somehow using the boards so that no part of the body touched the ground. Because there were two boards and they had two feet the children soon hit on the idea of using the boards as stepping stones. They stood on one board and moved the other ahead and then stepped on that and moved the first board ahead. This was an effective way of getting across the room.

A second group of children were only given one of the boards and the piece of string. After a while a few of them tied the string to the hole in the board. Then they stood on the board and holding it up against their feet with the string they hopped across the room. This was a much better way of getting across the room than the stepping stone method. But the children with two boards were completely unable to find this solution since they were blocked by the adequacy of the other solution. This process is shown as a d-line diagram on page 286.

An approach may choose itself because it is obvious, or it may be the only one left after other approaches have been blocked with a NO label.

With vertical thinking, an approach is selected in either one of these two ways. With lateral thinking, as many alternatives as possible are generated. One disregards the NO reaction since so often it is applied prematurely. One may recognize the obvious approach but nevertheless go on generating other ones as well.

In the example shown previously (page 251) there would have been no difficulty if the person arranging the plastic pieces had not been satisfied with the adequate rectangle arrangement but had gone on to generate other arrangements such as the square.

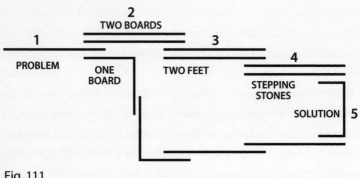

Fig. 111

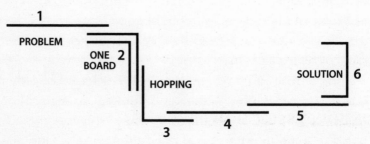

Fig. 112

NON-SEQUENTIAL

There may be no reason for saying something until after it has been said. Once it has been said a context develops to support it, and yet it would never have been produced by a context. It may not be possible to plan a new style in art, but once it has come about it creates its own validity. It is usual to proceed forward step by step until one has got somewhere. But it is also possible to get there first by any means and then look back and find the best route. A problem may be worked forward from the beginning but it may also be worked backwards from the end.

Instead of proceeding steadily along a pathway one jumps to a different point, or several different points, in turn and then waits for them to link together to give a coherent pattern. It is in the nature of the self-maximizing system of the memory-surface to create a coherent pattern out of such separate points. If the pattern is effective then it cannot possibly matter whether it came about in a sequential fashion or not. A frame of reference is a context provided by the current arrangement of information. It is the direction of development implied by this arrangement. One cannot break out of this frame of reference by working from within it. It may be necessary to jump out, and if the jump is successful then the frame of reference is itself altered.

UNDOING SELECTION PROCESSES

Lateral thinking seeks to avoid the selecting processes of natural thinking and logical thinking in order to find out whether a useful arrangement has been excluded by such selection processes. Thus no attention is paid to either the negative blocking of logical thinking or the dominant attraction of natural thinking selection.

In logical thinking each step must be justified, otherwise it would be blocked with a negative. In lateral thinking the steps do not have to be justified. One can proceed through an area that might have been labelled wrong. It might turn out that the label was prematurely applied (as with the spiral cut in the postcard). It might turn out that the label was valid when it was applied but is no longer so. It might turn out that the correct pathway is only visible from a point beyond the wrong area which itself drops out of the eventual pathway. A bridge does not have to be justified or self-supporting at every stage in its building so long as it is self-supporting at the end.

Lateral thinking also seeks to break down the natural self-selection of cliché units or patterns that have been built up on the memory-surface. It may be a matter of cutting across these units and re-creating new units. It may be a matter of distorting an obvious pattern in order to let a new one emerge. Anything that is fixed, accepted or taken for granted can be re-examined in an attempt to set free the information imprisoned within it or to remove the blocking effect it might be having.

There is an operations research story about the skyscraper that was built with too few lifts. As a result the office staff became impatient with the delays and began to leave. The architects and the engineers suggested putting in more lift shafts to speed up the movement of staff but declared that this would be costly. The operations research people had a simpler solution. They put mirrors around the lift entrances, with the result that the staff were so occupied with their reflections that they were no longer impatient. Here the simple solution depended on moving from the obvious cliché pattern of speeding up the movement of staff, to removing their impatience.

ATTENTION

Any established pattern on the memory-surface has a natural attention sequence. An alteration in this attention sequence can make the flow of activation not only proceed in a different direction along the same path but actually follow a different path. This mechanism was discussed in the section on insight, since it could be the basis both of insight solution to problems and of insight learning.

A man gets into the lift in his office building every morning, proceeds to the tenth floor then gets out and walks up to the sixteenth floor. At night he gets in to the lift outside his office and gets out on the ground floor. What might the man be up to? Most people suggest that he is a keep-fit fiend and likes the daily exercise of walking up six floors. Others suggest that he does not want to be seen by someone who might be taking the lift from any of the last six floors. Or else he might be late each morning and the lift entrance is opposite his employer's office and the stair entrance is not. In fact the man was very short, and could not reach higher than the tenth floor button of the lift.

A friend of mine claimed to smuggle handbags in from Paris by filling them with cheap scent on which she was duly asked to pay duty. No one noticed that the handbags themselves were always new.

While changing a wheel a man lost all five of the securing nuts, which vanished down a road drain. He had no idea what to do and set about thumbing a lift to the nearest garage. A little boy happened to be passing by and asked what the matter was. When he was told he said, 'Oh, that's easy, you just take one nut each from the other wheels and that should see you to a garage.'

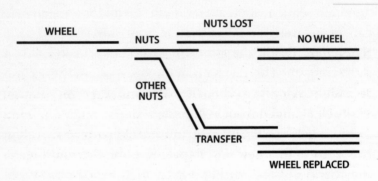

Fig. 113

In each of these cases a slight shift of attention changes the whole pattern of the situation: a shift from what the man in the lift does to what he is capable of doing; a shift from the contents of the bag to the container itself; a shift from the wheel that cannot be put onto the availability of nuts as nuts. The effect of this last shift of attention is shown in d-line form above.

USE OF LATERAL THINKING

Although lateral thinking can often be recognized only after it has brought something about, this does not mean that it is impossible to use it deliberately. The practical use of lateral thinking involves simple fixed techniques, an awareness of the limitations of ordinary information-processing and a more general device which will be dealt with later.

The simple fixed techniques or algorithms are as definite as mathematical algorithms. They are pre-set patterns which are learned and then used with different information.

RANDOM INPUT

In a self-maximizing system the patterns that evolve cannot easily be changed from within the system. A random input from outside can serve to disrupt the old pattern and allow it to reform in a new way. Exposure to random influences may be as general as walking through a supermarket or an exhibition, or as definite as opening a dictionary and selecting a page and a word at random. In each case attention moves from the random input to the problem in hand and back again in an oscillation. Given the nature of the memory-surface there must eventually arise a linking pattern and from this linking pattern may arise a new point of entry into the original problem and new ideas about it. The production of the random input is quite deliberate, the use made of it depends on the properties of the memory-surface.

QUOTA

It is quite easy to set up a fixed quota of alternative approaches that must be found for any problem. No one approach is followed until the quota has been filled. This procedure will not itself generate new approaches but it will keep attention at the starting-point instead of letting it be led away by the first promising approach to the extent that other approaches are never looked for.

ROTATION OF ATTENTION

If one divides the situation up into parts then it is possible to have a deliberate technique which requires that each part in rotation becomes the centre of attention. Once again this is a delaying technique to prevent attention being monopolized by the most dominant feature.

REVERSAL

This involves taking something and turning it upside down. Where one direction is defined then the opposite direction is also defined by implication.

In a winding country lane a motorist came up behind a slow-moving flock of sheep which filled the lane from side to side. The lane was bounded by high walls with no gap and the motorist was resigned to a long wait. Then the shepherd signalled the motorist to stop, and proceeded to turn the flock round and drive it back past the stationary motorist.

It was a matter of getting the sheep past the car rather than getting the car past the sheep.

CROSS-FERTILIZATION

This is a matter of providing a formal opportunity for different minds to interact so that differences in thinking about a subject act as outside influences to change the established patterns in each mind. What is established in one mind may be novel in another. Ideas spark off other ideas.

These are a few of the formal techniques that can be used in lateral thinking. The techniques provide special opportunities for lateral thinking processes to occur on the memory-surface. Just as a scientific experiment is a designed opportunity for information to become manifest, so the formal techniques are opportunities for information to become arranged in new patterns. The patterns will be different, some of them may be better.

Lateral thinking is a generative type of thinking. Once a new arrangement of information has come about then it can be examined by the usual selective processes. Lateral thinking as a process can never justify the outcome, which has to stand by itself. Lateral thinking in no way detracts from the efficiency of vertical thinking. On the contrary, as a generative process it can only add to the over-all effectiveness of any selective process.

It sometimes happens that lateral thinking can provide an insight rearrangement of information that by itself solves the problem. At other times lateral thinking provides an approach for vertical thinking to develop.

CHAPTER 34

PO

PO is a new word. PO makes possible a type of thinking that would be impossible without it. PO is made necessary by the deficiencies of the special memory-surface.

PO is to lateral thinking what NO is to logical thinking. Lateral thinking could be regarded as the management of PO just as logical thinking is the management of NO.

The defects of the special memory-surface may be summarized here. The surface records information by processing it into discrete units which become more and more firmly established until these polarizing units actually determine what information is accepted. The units come to be arranged in patterns which get more and more firmly established until they themselves act as rigid cliché patterns which can no longer be broken down into their component parts. Both these processes follow from the nature of the surface, which merely provides an opportunity for information to organize itself. Information does organize itself to give a pattern which is the best arrangement at the time. The nature of the surface tends to establish such patterns ever more firmly. In any case the patterns tend to be self-perpetuating, since they control attention. The result is that the patterns persist even though they are no longer the best possible arrangement of available information. Since the sequence of arrival plays so important a part in the arrangement of information, this must always be less than the best possible arrangement, which should depend on the information alone. Because they control attention these imperfect patterns are not easily changed. Occasionally, however, a chance combination of circumstances in the environment will trigger off a complete re-structuring of the arrangement of information so that this gets closer to the best possible arrangement. This is the insight phenomenon. An example of this phenomenon is the finding of an obvious solution to an apparently difficult problem. Often the solution is only obvious after it has been found.

There are two aspects of this inherent limitation in the handling of information by a self-organizing memory-surface. The first aspect is the necessity to proceed by steps which can only reflect experience, which may be first- or second-hand. Abstractions or combinations of separate experiences are possible, but they remain experience-dominated. The collection of new information is also experience-dominated, since new information is only selected if it fits in with existing patterns – relevance is all-important. This natural behaviour of the surface has been accentuated by education, which will only permit thinking to take place in justified sequential steps. To enforce this, education teaches the use of the effective NO device.

The second aspect of the inherent limitation of a self-organizing memory-surface is the way the organization of information is cumulative. Past information controls what happens to new information. Patterns are created, become established and grow ever more rigid. In its pattern-making, the memory-surface has a divisive tendency which makes divisions where none exist, and which separates things into fixed categories; and from this follows the polarizing tendency which looks only at extremes. Sometimes this polarizing tendency makes minor differences into major ones, and at other times it fails to recognize major differences as it pushes things into established patterns. Once again education reinforces these tendencies by means of the 'labelling' device which freezes established patterns and divisions. Of particular importance is the NO label, with its rigid exclusion. The result of these tendencies is an arrogance and rigidity of pattern which is quite unjustified by the information contained.

The two functions of the PO device match these two aspects of the inherent limitation of the memory-surface. The first function of PO is to treat as true patterns of information for which there is no justification in experience – in order to allow insight re-structuring and the generation of new ideas. The second function of PO is to lessen the arrogant truth of a particular point of view and so free information – in order to allow insight restructuring and the generation of new ideas. Both functions emphasize the usefulness of temporary patterns of information but the danger of rigid patterns. Although these two functions of PO are really the same thing they are discussed in detail under separate headings for the sake of convenience.

THE FIRST USE OF PO

There are two quite distinct ways in which thinking can establish useful conclusions.

1. The first way involves careful step-by-step extension of what is already known until eventually a new conclusion is reached. This is logical or mathematical thinking. The soundness of the conclusion is proved by the soundness of the pathway by which it has been reached.

2. The second way involves the exploratory rearrangement of what is known by disrupting accepted patterns and generating new ones. Any process whatsoever that will bring this about is used. When a useful rearrangement has come about it must make sense on its own. In contrast to the first method, the new conclusion can never depend for its soundness on the way it has come about. From the new conclusion it may be possible to look back to the starting-point and rationalize a perfectly sound logical pathway to support the conclusion. If the pathway is sound then it cannot possibly matter from which end it was constructed. Because a sound logical pathway can be constructed once the conclusion has been reached does not mean that the conclusion would have been reached by this pathway.

The difference between the two methods is shown in the picture on page 298.

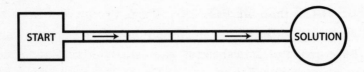

Fig. 114

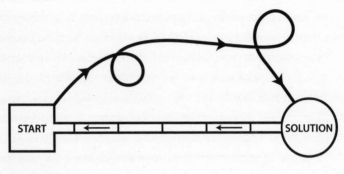

Fig. 115

THE END BEFORE THE MEANS

One may have to be at the top of a mountain in order to find the best way up. There may not be a reason for saying something until after it has been said. A solution may be obvious only after it has been found. But how does one get to the top of the mountain first? PO is a cheat device which enables one to get there by allowing information to be used in ways which are completely unjustified by experience. Without PO one has to start at the foot of the mountain and climb upwards by careful steps, each step being fully justified.

To start at the end instead of at the beginning is a well-known problem-solving technique. It often works, because starting at the end gives one a fresh entry point into the problem. In the section on insight, in Chapter 23, the huge importance of a fresh entry point was deduced from the mechanics of information-handling on the special memory-surface. If the problem has a defined end point then it is hardly necessary to use PO in order to start from this end point. But if the problem is open-ended then it is necessary to generate an end point, and PO is very useful for this purpose.

The generated end point may make sense, or it may not. Suppose the problem was one of overcrowding. A generated end point might be, 'Po people should live inside one another.' This is nonsensical in itself but it could lead on to such ideas as, '... not actually within each other's skin, but in the same space – why should a person have a permanent occupation of a space he only uses occasionally? Perhaps one could have a shift system with high utilization of living space or working space.'

With PO one can generate entry points anywhere along the way. Even in closed problems one does not have to go to the defined end point as the only alternative to the starting-point. In considering the problem of transport within cities one might suggest, 'Po why not transport stomachs and eyes instead of whole people.'

DISCONNECTED JUMPS

If one is proceeding by justified steps along a sequential pathway one may get blocked, or run out of progress, or one may find oneself going round in circles. In all these circumstances it can be very useful to make a jump to a new point. It has to be a jump because one is not able to make any sequential progress. PO can act as the link, as the justification for making the jump. In effect PO indicates that one is not making the jump out of caprice but because the information-processing behaviour of the mind demands it. By means of PO one can say anything one likes, without it having to have any relevance to the problem, and still remain within the problem context. Because the memory-surface tends to link things up, whatever is said will develop a relevance to the problem and perhaps help towards its solution.

Suppose the problem being discussed was the desirability of student participation in university affairs, and one person broke off to say, 'Po the cat had kittens.' This might stimulate such ideas as '... over-reaction to demands – splitting up of main demand into antagonistic minor ones – life goes on – kittens are blind at birth but develop quickly – kittens need protection and feeding – one idea breeds others – cats are but ornaments anyway.' To be useful, the jump does not have to be so outrageous. A simpler jump like, 'Po the university finances are low', might have had some effect.

Apart from the single jump one can proceed scattily from one idea to another unconnected idea, using PO as the sole link. This is usually more useful for generating ideas than for solving specific problems.

JUXTAPOSITION

PO can be used to bring things together in a completely neutral manner. PO neither affirms ('is' function) nor denies ('not' function) nor adds ('and' function) nor alternates ('or' function). Unlike these other words it is not intended to bring about an arrangement of words that makes sense in itself but an arrangement that triggers off something else. The most fantastic and unlikely things can be put together in this way.

'Po the moon is made of green cheese.' This could trigger off such ideas as the following: 'The moon is as familiar an object as cheese but has always been remote – it may become as accessible as cheese. It does not matter what the moon is made of, it is the symbolic nature of the moon that matters and scientific proof of its nature tends to destroy the magic rather than enhance it. Perhaps the moon could be a source of food, not as a substance but as a special type of farming area for synthetic foods. The great efforts to reach the moon were not worth the bother – it would only help world starvation if it were made of green cheese. Remote and mysterious things may be quite commonplace. Today one could actually obtain a piece of moon and examine it – the speed of technological progress may soon make it possible to examine other uncheckable fancies. The moon would be more interesting if it were made of green cheese – what use could the substance of the moon be?'

The ideas that are triggered off by this statement are not especially useful. But a statement of this sort does seem to trigger off more ideas than saying, 'The moon is covered with dust.'

REVERSAL

PO can be used to turn things upside down. Consider the statement, 'Thinking is a matter of selecting material and processing it into increasingly regular patterns.' This makes sense, but consider a reversal of the statement, 'Po thinking involves decreasing the regularity of patterns.' From this reversal arises the idea of lateral thinking, and the disruption of regularity in order to allow information to re-form into new patterns.

Reversal is an easy process since whenever a direction is implied the opposite direction is also implied. This makes it one of the more reliable ways of producing a disruptive stimulus.

There was once a rich man who wanted his daughter to marry one of her rich suitors. He forbade her to see the poor student with whom she was in love. The daughter knew about lateral thinking so she said to herself, 'Po Daddy actually paid this poor student to marry me!' From this absurd suggestion came an idea. She went to her father and said she wanted to marry the richest of her suitors. To find out which one was the richest she suggested her father should give a large present to each suitor. They would then be able to tell how rich each was by the difference the present made to his way of life. In order to see if the method was valid the present would be given to each of the suitors, including the poor student. The presents were given. And the daughter eloped with the now enriched student.

BEING WRONG

In the course of evolution it may be necessary to have a few dud species in order to evolve a highly effective one. In the evolution of ideas it may be necessary to go through a wrong stage in order to arrive at a useful idea. The most fundamental difference between lateral thinking and vertical thinking is that in vertical thinking one is not allowed to be wrong at any stage, whereas in lateral thinking one is allowed to be wrong on the way to the solution. Being wrong may be necessary in order to get information together in a certain way which can then develop into a useful solution. The solution itself must be correct, but it may be necessary to be wrong in order ever to get there.

There is also the possibility that one is wrong only in the current frame of reference. It is by being prepared to be wrong that the frame of reference itself eventually gets to be changed.

PO is a device which enables one to be wrong without having to try to justify it. In this way one is allowed to proceed through a wrong area on the way to a correct solution. Used in this fashion PO may also shift emphasis onto the frame of reference within which the statement seems to be wrong.

Since a large part of a ship's time is spent unprofitably at the dock-side while it is loaded and unloaded, one might be considering the problem of developing new loading methods such as the use of containers. Then someone might suggest, 'Po why shouldn't ships be loaded in the docks while they are still at sea.' This seems quite wrong, and yet it could lead on to a consideration of total loading and unloading units which could be processed while the propulsion, crew and navigating functions of the ship were still at sea. Here the frame of reference has been changed from consideration of how to load and unload a ship while it is at the dock to the design of the ship itself.

SEMI-CERTAINTY

A catalyst enables a chemical reaction to take place but does not form part of the final product. The catalyst performs its function and then drops out, and yet without the catalyst the reaction would never have come about. The function of the catalyst is to hold things in the right position for interaction to take place. A vitamin is not a food, but it enables the body to use food. Catalysts, vitamins and enzymes are communication points which allow chemicals to interact with each other. That is also the function that PO performs with regard to information.

Quite often one comes to the point where one thinks. 'If only this were true then I could proceed. It seems true but I cannot prove it just yet.' In these circumstances PO allows one to proceed – in thought, not in action – as if it were true. By proceeding one may get to a point where the truth of the statement can be proved. Or one may get to a point where the doubtful statement is found to be unnecessary and can be dropped out. Or one may find that the ultimate structure is useful in its own right no matter how unsound the process by which it came about. PO reinforces the doubtful statement enough to allow one to proceed but not enough to make it support the final conclusion.

One needs something like PO in these circumstances, for otherwise one must either come to a stop or else proceed as if the statement were true with nothing tangible to show that the truth is only provisional. This particular use of PO is very close to the ordinary use of hypothesis and 'suppose'.

CONSTRUCTION

This use of PO is like the use of a construction in school geometry. For instance, if one has to prove that a line parallel to the base of a triangle and bisecting one side must also bisect the other side then one can use the construction shown on page 306. In effect something is brought in from outside. The situation is changed in a manner that is not inherent within the situation.

A philosopher climbs to the top of a mountain to meditate. He starts at dawn and gets there by nightfall. He spends the night on top of the mountain but falls asleep and does not wake until early afternoon the next day. He starts down the mountainside and gets home by nightfall. How can one show that there may be some spot on the mountainside which he reaches at exactly the same time of day on both the way up and the way down?

It is possible to work out this simple problem with graphs and so on. But one could more easily say, 'Po the philosopher coming down the mountain meets himself going up.' When they meet they must be at the same spot at the same time.

Once the rearrangement of information has taken place to give the solution then the construction can drop away, just as the scaffolding is removed when the bridge supports itself.

RANDOM STIMULUS

One of the basic principles of lateral thinking is that a random stimulus from outside may be required in order to

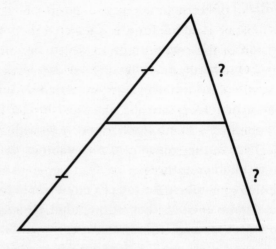

Fig. 116

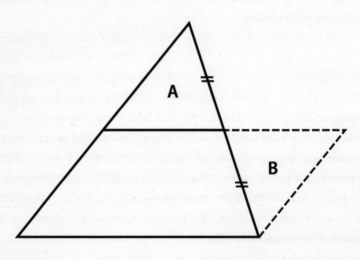

Fig. 117

re-structure a pattern or change a point of view. The stimulus must be random, for if it is selected then it is only an extension of the current pattern which will merely be reinforced. One hardly needs the PO device in order to use a random stimulus for one can just go ahead and use one. The function of PO is to formalize the procedure, to indicate that the stimulus is being deliberately used as a random stimulus. Thus in the course of a discussion on crime the participants might be rather perplexed if someone suddenly said 'chewing gum'. But if he were to say, 'Po chewing gum' then it would be obvious what he intended. The formality imparted by PO makes the random stimulus technique easier to use without embarrassment. In effect PO implies that a random stimulus may be needed at this point in order to generate some new approaches. PO converts what might otherwise be taken as madness into a perfectly reasonable illogical procedure.

SUMMARY

The first function of PO is simply to enable one to say anything one wants, not because it makes sense in itself, but because it can lead to a rearrangement of information that does make sense in itself. When a particular use of information is not justified by experience, by relevance or by logic, then PO is a device which justifies it temporarily. Some of the specific uses of PO have been listed, but other uses can be devised once one realizes the basic function of the word.

THE SECOND USE OF PO

The second function of PO is to diminish the rigidity of the patterns that inevitably form on the special memory-surface. It is in the nature of the surface to create and use such patterns. From a biological point of view the more rigid the pattern the better. From a social point of view rigidity may not be an advantage.

ANTI-ARROGANCE

It is in the nature of the special memory-surface to form self-perpetuating patterns that seem uniquely true. PO acts as a reminder that the rigidity of the pattern depends on the nature of the memory-surface and not on the unique validity of the particular pattern that has formed. A training in the use of PO could temper the arrogance of the fierce, dogmatic attitudes that become ever more set through use and opposition. A realization of the arbitrary nature and historical development of such attitudes still leaves them useful but can remove the arrogance that precludes other points of view and even insists that others should hold the same point of view.

PO is but a can-opener. It does not empty the contents of the can. PO does not disprove a point of view. What PO indicates is, 'You may be right, what you hold may be very useful, but remember that it is in the nature of the memory-surface to create rigid self-perpetuating patterns that seem uniquely true.'

Arrogance appears in many forms. Just as one particular fixed way of looking at things leads to the arrogance of pride, so another fixed way of looking at things leads to the arrogance of despair. PO can be used to temper the arrogance of despair by suggesting that things may not be as bad as they seem to be, or that they might not be so permanently bad as they seem. The use of PO not as a temporary device but as an attitude of mind can take the edge off such arrogance.

It is not suggested that PO should be used so fiercely that one loses all effectiveness. It is not suggested that the realization of the arbitrariness of patterns should lead to a loss of drive and direction. On the contrary, one realizes that patterns are extremely useful, no matter how arbitrary, and so one uses them. But uses them without arrogance, with an inquiry about better patterns and with the willingness to change to better patterns if they should seem more useful. PO itself stops one being arrogant about the use of PO.

Humour follows from the same basic mechanics on the special memory-surface as does insight. Both indicate the possibility of alternative arrangements of information in addition to the established pattern. In its reminder of the behaviour of the memory-surface PO suggests the same things as a sense of humour, a sense of proportion and tolerance for another point of view (but not necessarily tolerance for the rigidity of another point of view).

PO AS INTERJECTION

If someone makes a statement with which you do not agree you might simply say NO at the end – or some more polite version. If someone makes a statement as the only possible truth then you might say PO at the end. This does not mean that there is anything wrong with the statement except its arrogance. Used in this way PO may indicate that the statement is perfectly correct within its frame of reference but that the frame of reference may itself be wrong. PO also implies, 'I cannot find fault with your statement, nor can I offer an alternative one just now. Nevertheless it is a particular way of looking at the situation and there may be other and better ones. I shall accept your statement provisionally – as useful but not as unique.'

Whereas NO implies categorical disagreement, PO implies disagreement not with the contents of the statement but with the dogma of it. PO is an inducement to keep in mind the errors in the information-processing system of the special memory-surface.

RE-UNITE

One of the characteristic features of the memory-surface is the dividing of things into separate units which then grow farther apart. The division of the process of change into 'cause' and 'effect' was given as an example of this.

PO attacks the divisions temporarily in order to let information be used in a different way. PO may also be used simply to indicate the arbitrariness of the division. Sometimes it may be the whole division that is arbitrary, at other times the division is useful on one level but arbitrary if carried through to other levels. In the latter case PO may seem to be pleading for attention to what unites the fragments rather than what divides them. If so, this is a by-product. The function of PO is only to challenge the rigidity of a division.

If one were to say, 'men po women', this would be the same as saying 'people' or 'humanity'. It would, however, be very different from saying, 'men and women', since this deliberately keeps them distinct in order to add them together – whereas PO gets rid of the distinction. There would be a difference between saying, 'Democrat po Republican', and saying, 'Democrat and Republican'. The former would indicate that the differences might not be very basic and the latter would suggest both separate points of view. 'Government po people' would focus attention on whether there was any common interest between the two. PO itself is never a judgment – it is a device for challenging divisions. 'Rich po poor' does not mean that there is no basic difference between rich and poor but means, 'Let us look at this division, evaluate it, and see what happens if we drop it for the moment.' The challenged division may crumble under the challenge or it may stand up to it, in which case the juxtaposition may become stimulating in its own right.

Consider two different uses of PO:

1. Battleships po puppy dogs.
2. Northerners po Southerners.

In the first instance the two things are put together because experience would be unlikely to put them together. In the second instance the two things are put together because experience has shoved them apart. Both uses run counter to experience and the purpose in both cases is stimulation.

In challenging the division PO may bridge it temporarily in order to see if anything useful can emerge. For instance in an industrial dispute an attitude of 'workers po employers' might lead to consideration of such common interests as productivity or to ideas like workers' participation. 'Love po hate' leads on to a consideration of the basic force of reaction that is manifest in both and to the Freudian idea that the two are not so distinct.

In this uniting function PO is especially useful in bringing together those opposite extremes which are created by one another. Thus flexible is created as an opposite to rigid, and the other way round. Yet a 'flexible po rigid' system is what everyone is looking for. This also applies to 'tough po humble' and 'chaos po control', as suggested in an earlier section.

The reunited fragments are not meant to be treated as permanent structures but only to trigger off ideas. The link-up is temporary, otherwise the useful function of language to create separate mobile units would be lost. One does not want to lose the distinctness of 'rigid' and 'flexible' but to keep it and still show that a system can be both of these things at once. It is the division and separateness that is attacked by PO, and not the nature of the two qualities.

COUNTERACTING NO

Just as PO can be used to challenge divisions and temporarily to remove labels, so it can be used to counteract that most effective of all labels, the NO label. The NO reaction is so well trained into thinking habits that one of the most necessary functions of PO is to unblock pathways which have at some time been blocked by the NO label (perhaps a very long time ago). As usual, PO does not judge the validity of the label but merely sets it aside temporarily to allow the blocked information to be used again.

This function of counteracting the NO label can be very useful since NO is so powerful a blocking device. The NO label may have been applied prematurely. It may have been valid at the time of application but is no longer so. The label may still be valid, but information locked away under it may now be useful in some other context. Science is always looking back and finding great usefulness in ideas that had been rejected or thrown out because at the time of judgment they did not make sense.

Once the NO label has been attached then it remains permanently attached, because of the emotional nature of the NO reaction. And since the NO sign hangs at the very entrance to the path this cannot even be explored to see if the sign is still applicable.

PO only counteracts the NO label temporarily. Usually the block recurs because it is indeed justified. There are times, however, when the block does not recur once it has been removed. Until the early sixties, most art critics would have regarded a can of soup as non-art. Then Andy Warhol painted his famous can of soup and it suddenly became art. Once the block had been removed a context developed which prevented the block ever coming back.

ALTERNATIVE APPROACHES

In addition to unblocking pathways, PO can be used to block pathways. More dangerous than a blocked pathway is capture by a promising pathway. After all, a block makes you look elsewhere, but a capture prevents you looking anywhere else. Being captured by the adequate, being captured by the obvious, both prevent the best use of information. An approach achieves a natural dominance through familiarity, emotional content or because it leads somewhere. PO is used to block temporarily the naturally dominant approach. In effect PO indicates, 'This approach may be all right but it may not be the most effective one. Let's leave it for the moment and try and find others.' This is a different sort of block to the NO block since PO is always temporary.

The statement, 'Nora is ugly', may have a natural obviousness but if one blocks this as with, 'Po Nora is not ugly', then one might be able to consider the worth of individual features which previously were swamped by the over-all judgment.

In the experiment with the children and the two boards the more effective solution could have been found by the first group if they had said to themselves, 'Po the stepping-stones method is not the only way of doing this.'

Lister has been given much credit for the development of modern surgery through his introduction of carbolic acid as a disinfectant. Lawson Tait thought Lister was talking a lot of nonsense, and he himself obtained excellent results not by using disinfectant but by being scrupulously clean. In fact modern surgery uses this aseptic method and not the antiseptic one. Po killing bacteria is not the only way of preventing them from infecting wounds.

SUMMARY

The second function of PO is as a freeing device to free one from the rigidity of established ideas, patterns, labels, divisions, categories and classifications. PO is a tool for de-patterning. While acknowledging the necessity for patterns and their tremendous usefulness it is convenient to have some method of questioning the rigidity of these patterns and even disrupting them temporarily. PO acts as a reminder of the pattern-forming behaviour of the memory-surface. As a reminder, PO tempers the arrogance of a particular point of view.

Even if PO is never actually used, an awareness of the nature of this device can serve to lessen the rigidity of mind.

EMOTIONAL CONTENT OF PO

Since the special memory-surface is a passive self-organizing system, the NO reaction could never alter what happened on the surface unless NO had an emotional content. NO acts as the symbolic anticipation of a situation that would arouse pain or discomfort. The pain may be physical, and this may be the case with early training in the use of NO. There is probably also a purely intellectual discomfort which is aroused by a mis-match situation. With perception this mis-match can give rise to nausea when something seems to be two different things at once.

The emotional content of PO would be derived from the anticipation of the pleasure of an insight solution or a eureka moment when everything suddenly snaps into place. This pleasure is related to that of humour, and possibly even that of aesthetic appreciation. In each case there is the sudden establishment of an easy pattern as opposed to the awkward conflict of a mis-match situation. This type of emotional response could also be related to hope, which is an anticipation that things will work out, and to curiosity and exploration.

PO could also derive some emotional content from the diminution of the fearsomeness of rigid ways of looking at a situation. The ultimate effect of the emotional content of PO is that it enables PO to establish connections that are not mere reflections of experience, just as NO acts to weaken connections that are reflections of experience.

Both the unpleasant reaction and the pleasant reaction are mechanical processes on the memory-surface, and have nothing to do with the value content of the information. Thus the instability of the mis-match situation could lead to an oscillation in the general activity of the surface, while the pleasant reaction may lead to a reduction in this oscillatory activity. The actual mechanical nature of the reaction is unimportant, but it must be something to do with the way the surface is behaving and not to do with the actual information on the surface.

HYPOTHESIS, SUPPOSE, POETRY

It might seem that the function of PO is already covered by the above words. There is some degree of overlap, and there might be a tendency for the natural polarizing property of mind to exaggerate this overlap and conclude that PO serves no new function.

'Hypothesis' means the most reasonable guess at the moment. It is not yet 'proved', but it is reasonably derived from the current arrangement of knowledge and the intention is to prove it in due course. In sharp contrast, the function of PO is to be as unreasonable as possible and even to be as far as possible from the current arrangement of knowledge in order to have a disruptive effect. PO is provocative. There is no intention of proving the PO statement to be correct.

'Suppose' is similar in function to 'if ', and both permit the use of a statement which is not yet justified. But both deal with events that are quite reasonable in themselves; the only unreasonable thing about them is that they are described as if they have happened when in fact they have not. In a very much weaker way 'suppose' could fulfil some of the functions of PO, but the effect would be different. To say, 'Suppose the moon were made of green cheese', is not the same as saying, 'Po the moon is made of green cheese'. The juxtaposition, random stimulation and reuniting functions of PO could not be carried out by 'suppose'. The weakness of 'suppose' is that it is still working from within the system and therefore cannot achieve the disrupting effect of PO which is working against the system. The function of PO as a freeing device is not based on reasonable doubt but on unreasonable doubt.

Perhaps the nearest equivalent is poetry. In poetry are put together things that may be nonsense with the intention of provoking a new way of looking at the situation. Words are used in extraordinary ways. All this is much nearer to the function of PO.

GRAMMATICAL USE OF PO

PO can be used in any way that seems natural. Since PO is never intended to be an excuse for telling lies, any statement covered by PO must be clearly seen to be covered by PO. The examples given throughout this chapter give some indication of how PO is used.

1. At the beginning of a statement that is to be covered by PO.
   PO can also be used before any particular phrase or word that is to be qualified and need not apply to the whole statement, e.g.:
   This new word is po a dangerous word to use.

2. PO can be used as a link between two words or concepts to challenge the division that separates them. It can also be used in this position to form a stimulating juxtaposition, e.g.:
   Artists po intellectuals will find the new word easy to use.

3. PO can be used in most positions in which 'no' or 'not' can be used. This includes the use of PO as a simple response to a statement, e.g.:
   There is a definite need for this new word.
   Po!

4. PO can be used to counteract the effect of NO. For this purpose the statement is rephrased as a positive statement qualified by PO in the usual way, e.g.:
   A new word cannot be artificially put into use.
   Po a new word can be artificially put into use.

PO AND LANGUAGE

It is unlikely that the full function of PO would evolve naturally in any language since the function is directly opposed to the nature of language. Whereas language either as communication or as an aid to thought seeks to be discriminatory and sequential, PO seeks exactly the opposite. Language is concerned with the mobility of patterns that must themselves be fixed and stable in order to achieve any meaning. PO is a challenge to the stability of these fixed patterns. *The whole purpose of PO is to provide a temporary escape from the discrete and ordered stability of language which reflects the fixed patterns of a self-organizing memory-system.* PO is a laxative to counteract the constipating effects of language.

SUMMARY

Our culture and education are concerned with establishing and communicating ideas. There is no method for changing ideas except conflict. Lateral thinking is necessary for the internal re-structuring of ideas. PO is suggested as a practical tool for putting lateral thinking into effect. PO is an insight tool.

Just as the negative is the basis of logical thinking so the (re)laxative is the basis of lateral thinking. PO is the laxative.

Apart from its use, PO is of value as a symbol of the inherent limitation of information-handling on the special memory-surface.

CHAPTER 35

PHYSIOLOGY

This book has been concerned with building up, principle by principle, a type of information-processing system. This system has been capable of such things as the direction of attention and thinking. It has also been shown that there are certain inherent errors in the information-processing behaviour of this type of system, just as there are certain tremendous advantages. The advantages by far outweigh the disadvantages, even though more attention has been paid to the latter. The system has been called a special memory-surface, and it is activity on this surface that has been described.

Throughout there has been an obvious assumption that this type of system may be similar to the one operating in the human brain. At times this assumption may have progressed too far from possibility towards certainty for the comfort of many readers. This was a matter of convenience, since it is extremely awkward to write continuously in tentative terms. At this point it may be repeated that what has been described is a type of system. Whether in broad terms this system is the one operating in the brain remains to be proved. What is known about the brain does support in broad terms a system of this sort. The details may be very different. There follows a brief summary of relevant features.

TRANSLATION

It is known that a pattern presented to the eye or ear will evoke a response on the surface of the brain. In this book it has been assumed that somehow the presented patterns arrive on the memory-surface without any consideration of how they get there. The processes of getting things there, the process of translating an object in the environment into a pattern on the brain surface is very complex. This translation may itself carry out quite a lot of information-processing.

INHIBITION AND EXCITATION

Most of the characteristic behaviour of the special memory-surface depends on the interaction of inhibition and excitation. From a balance between these arises the limited area of activation that flits over the memory-surface directing attention. The balance between inhibition and excitation is a very fundamental and a very well-known characteristic of the nervous system. The processes may be effected by the interaction of the nerve units themselves, or by means of chemicals which bathe the units. The smooth functioning of any nervous behaviour has been shown to depend on a balance between excitation and inhibition.

Local anaesthetics are chemicals that depress nervous activity and hence are used by dentists to kill pain. If such nerve depressants are injected into the bloodstream they do not cause a depression of the activity of the brain but, on the contrary, a great excitement which is manifest as convulsions or hallucinations. It seems likely that this is because they depress the inhibiting function in the brain and so leave the exciting function out of balance. A larger dose of the drug will depress the excitation too.

The balance between inhibition and excitation gives rise to the selective, self-organizing and self-maximizing properties of the special memory-surface. This effect of inhibition and excitation acting against each other to give selection is seen throughout the biological world. It probably accounts for cell differentiation and explains why a hand comes to look like a hand and a nose like a nose. In the plant kingdom a balance between inhibitory and excitatory hormones decides whether plant cells shall turn into roots or stems and which way they shall grow.

UNITS

The special memory-surface was considered to be made up of functionally connected units which were capable of two states: activated or non-activated. The main ingredient of the nervous system is a switch called the synapse which may be either activated or not activated. It is true that most of what is known about such switches has been obtained by study of synapses outside the brain. The ones in the brain may be different, but the basic behaviour is unlikely to be very different.

The activation or not of the synapses depends on the cumulative balance between the excitatory and inhibitory influences acting on the unit. If a synapse is activated then it helps to pass on the activation to functionally connected units. The synapses themselves are interconnected by nerves. There is also evidence for a tiring factor, so that a synapse which has been active may for a short while become more difficult to activate.

SHORT-TERM MEMORY

There is evidence in the brain for a two-stage memory system consisting of a short-term memory and a long-term memory. The short-term memory could possibly take the form of an increased ease of activation of a synapse after the tiring factor had worn off. It could also take the form of circuits of nervous activity which circled round and round in endless loops for some time after a pattern of synapses had been activated. There is a special method of depolarizing the brain which stops nervous activity in an area. If this method is applied to the surface of an animal brain soon after some event it can prevent that event being recorded in memory. If it is applied much later then the memory is not interfered with. This suggests that the short-term memory has to do with nerve activity but the long-term one does not.

LONG-TERM MEMORY

On the special memory-surface, long-term memory consisted in a lowering of the threshold of a unit each time it was activated. Functionally the same effect could be obtained if the memory-trace consisted of the growth of new connections onto a synapse, or even if there were separate memory cells. It could also be obtained by a chemical change in the synapse which made it more likely to respond to a certain pattern of stimulation. The over-all function is that the effect of a type of activation is to increase the subsequent likelihood of that type of activation.

PATTERNS ON THE SURFACE

On the special memory-surface a unique set of units constituted a unique pattern. For convenience it was assumed that such a pattern would occupy a discrete area on the surface. It was pointed out that functionally connected units could be scrambled up among other units, and that a unique pattern need not be a single area but could consist of activated units scattered all over the surface as long as they formed a functional unit through their connections.

Nor is it even necessary that this functional unit should consist of units that are connected in any special way to each other. The units could be connected by resonance effects. When a broadcast is made, everyone whose radio is tuned to that frequency picks up the message. This would form a pattern of active radio receivers if one had a bird's eye view and could see them. For a different station the pattern would be different because the broadcasting frequency would be different. In the same way a special frequency of activity which covered the whole nerve surface might activate a pattern of those cells which were tuned to that frequency. Memory might consist of a change in the tuning.

On the special memory-surface the patterns were, for the sake of convenience, taken to be patterns in space. It would not matter if they were patterns in time. Writing and painting are patterns in space. Speech and music are patterns in time. A television set converts a pattern in time into a pattern in space. A simple model can be made with a number of pendulums which are suspended from a board which is itself suspended. The pendulums are of different lengths. If the pendulums swing then they interact with each other and a pattern in time and space of wildly swinging and still pendulums appears. This pattern is characteristic of the arrangement. But if one pendulum is shortened then the pattern is permanently altered. The patterns on the memory-surface may be patterns of this sort and depend on space, frequency and interaction.

The d-lines used to represent activity on the special memory-surface were not meant to indicate that activity always flowed in a spatial manner. All the d-lines indicate is that if pattern A is followed by pattern B then that leaves the surface in such a state that pattern C will follow. These are then shown as linked d-lines.

PARALLEL SYSTEMS

The brain is probably not a single memory-surface, otherwise one might stop breathing or fall down if one's attention were caught by something. There are presumably parallel systems which can function on their own. At the same time these systems are loosely integrated into the whole.

DANGERS OF INTROSPECTION

The trouble with the brain is that it is too available for introspection. If a system predicted that when an object was stared at then the object would disappear, this would be held to be nonsense as this is contrary to common experience. And yet if an object is held fixed relative to the retina, so that the image always falls on the same part of the retina no matter how the eye moves, then the object does in fact break up and disappear.

The brain appears to recognize patterns in all sorts of positions and orientations. One takes this to mean that there is some complicated system for instant pattern recognition. Yet the recognition may be no more than a matter of slowly learning that a square in one area is the same as a square in another area with no inbuilt mechanism for instant recognition at all. Or perhaps one recognizes not the pattern but the movements one makes in looking at the pattern. The point is that things may not be as simple as they seem, but they need not be as complicated as they seem either.

BROAD FEATURES

What have been described in this book are the very broad features of a system which has the following characteristics:

1. A memory system which records things.
2. An iterative memory system which means that changes are cumulative.
3. A self-organizing system which enables it to produce its own patterns.

4. A self-maximizing system which gives it selection.
5. A two-stage memory system which gives it a combining function.
6. An internal bias which gives it individuality and adaptive behaviour.

These are all broad processes which probably do apply to the brain no matter how the actual processes are carried out. The behaviour of the system depends on the functional processes, not the operative details, though it would be necessary to know these details if one wanted to tamper with the system.

The danger with broad functional descriptions is that if they are broad enough to encompass a variety of possible details then they are too broad to be of any use. Does the consideration of the brain as a biased, two-stage, iterative, self-maximizing memory-surface offer anything useful? It may. In the first place it shows how such a system is capable of self-education, of very efficient information-processing, of attention, of thinking, of insight, of humour and of self. In the second place it shows that the information-processing in this type of system has certain inherent defects, and it suggests ways these defects might be remedied.

PO AND THE BRAIN

The purpose of PO is to bring about an arrangement of information that can then be useful in itself, even though the way it came about does not provide it with validity. It cannot yet be proved that the brain *must* work like the special memory-surface. It may not be possible to prove it for a long time, because even if one comes to understand the cellular details the organization may still prove elusive.

So one can say: Po the type of system operating in the special memory-surface is the type operating in the brain. That is an arrangement of information which may prove useful or stimulating in its own right.

SUMMARY

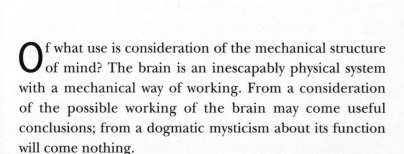

Of what use is consideration of the mechanical structure of mind? The brain is an inescapably physical system with a mechanical way of working. From a consideration of the possible working of the brain may come useful conclusions; from a dogmatic mysticism about its function will come nothing.

A few simple principles of behaviour can be put together to give a special memory-surface with four basic functions:

1. Separation and selection.
2. Combination and creation.
3. Extension.
4. Self-interest bias.

Together these functions provide a very useful information-processing system. This system is employed in the creation and evaluation of patterns, their establishment and subsequent recognition. The system is capable of both a gradual learning and insight learning. The behaviour of this simple memory-surface has processes analogous to consciousness, direction of attention, thinking and even humour. What this

shows is that a simple mechanical system is capable of processes that at first sight seem mysterious and elusive.

There is no switch which makes the memory-surface
handle important information in one way and trivial information in another. All information is treated in the same way
according to the characteristic behaviour of the system. The
behaviour of the system is characteristic enough to enable
one to expect certain things. For instance, the patterns on
the surface always tend to get larger and more firmly established. They become cliché patterns which offer increased
effectiveness in dealing with familiar situations, but much
less flexibility in dealing with new situations. Another characteristic is that there is no efficient mechanism for erasing
something that has been established on the surface. To erase
something one actually has to increase the emphasis but at
the same time make it lead to something unpleasant. In
effect one signposts the wrong direction even more clearly
than before but adds a warning to the signpost. This process
leads to the creation or use of the necessary myth of evil.

The self-maximizing nature of the system also means that
the edge of decision may be very fine. A very slight difference
between two alternatives may be quite sufficient for one of
them to be chosen and the other one completely ignored.
For the same reason a slight emotional emphasis in an otherwise natural situation can make the emphasized choice very
dominant over the unemphasized one. It is not a matter of
balancing the emphasis. Like driving in cross traffic, once
you get the nose of your car ever so slightly ahead then you
move across with confidence.

Learning is a matter of putting a new pattern onto the
surface or changing an established one. Ideally one would

let a pattern follow its natural development, and only pay attention to sensitive switch points to make sure that the direction of development was the one desired. This would be much more effective than trying to force the pattern onto the surface all the time. The huge importance of attention sequences both for learning and communication follows from the nature of the surface.

There is a suggestion that such phenomena as insight, humour, aesthetics and rhythm all depend on the same surface behaviour. All arise from the special information phenomenon which involves change and expectancy. The opposite phenomenon may account for the NO reaction, indecision and frustration which involve expectancy that is not matched by change. These things could be dealt with in terms of pure surface behaviour.

Any variation in all the different processes that make up the functioning of the surface would be reflected in that functioning. There might be variations in the strength of a process, such as the inhibiting effect that limits the area of activation, or there might be variations in the speed of certain processes, such as the tiring factor. These variations could lead to variations in surface behaviour that would be analogous to different levels of intelligence. Depending on the nature of the surface, the same rainfall might sculpt a smooth rounded landscape like the Sussex Downs or a sharp-edged ravine system like the Colorado Valley. It might one day be possible to measure intelligence by the rate of reaction of a particular enzyme system in a test-tube. For the same reasons the arguments between those who hold that there is a chemical basis for altered mental behaviour, and those who hold it to be a matter of unfortunate experience with incorrect pattern development, may be pointless. Chemical aberrations would override all others but the other aberrations could play a part even in the absence of chemical ones.

The most important thing that arises from a consideration of the information-handling in the type of system proposed is the nature of the errors and limitations which are inherent in the system. The very great efficiency of the system taken as a whole carries with it certain inherent faults.

Basically the system is very poor at updating itself. There is no efficient mechanism for doing this. In fact the accretion method of treating information inevitably leads to the arrangement of the information being slightly out of date. This is due to the importance of time of arrival of information and the persistence of established patterns. The arrangement of information on the memory-surface must always be less than the best possible arrangement. Humour is perhaps the most revealing of all intellectual functions, since it can only occur in this type of system. Problems for which the solutions are obvious only after they have been found and other insight *effects* also indicate the type of system. If the system has no efficient method for updating itself it certainly has no method at all for getting ahead of itself. Nor is this a necessary disadvantage. From a functional point of view adequacy is quite enough.

The more specific faults of the system include its divisive tendencies, which create artificial entities and artificial separations between them. This is the phenomenon that has been described as polarization. The memory-surface efficiently creates patterns out of the confused information offered it by the environment. But then these patterns take over, and instead of being a self-organization of available information they actually direct what information can be accepted. Once the patterns take over as cliché patterns or myths, then the prospects of changing such patterns are even more remote. Where the patterns are correct this is obviously an advantage, but where the patterns are imperfect it is another matter.

Leonardo da Vinci's diaries were lost for centuries for the simple reason that they were not lost at all. It seems that they had been mis-filed in some library. Had they been truly lost then there might have been a better chance of finding them. So it is with information that is incorrectly filed on the memory-surface by being fixed in a cliché pattern.

Once one is aware of the faults of the information-processing system one comes to realize that the main information sin is arrogance. Arrogance, dogmatism or a closed mind of any sort are so insecurely based on the fallible information-processing system that they would be pathetic if they were not sometimes dangerous.

For the same reasons the need to be always right, the insistence on this in education, and the basing of self-esteem on this need, cannot be justified unless it is tempered with the awareness that *for some part of the time one is inevitably going to be wrong.* It is these inherent faults of the information-processing system that make lateral thinking essential. Insight is so haphazard a mechanism that it cannot be expected to reduce the gap between the current arrangement of information and the best possible arrangement with any reliability. The purpose of lateral thinking is to bring about this insight type of re-structuring of information.

The sequential processes of vertical thinking as developed in logical and mathematical thinking are incredibly effective when one thinks how clumsy natural thinking is. Yet these sequential processes are not effective in bringing about the insight type of re-structuring of information. One cannot change a sequential pattern by developing it further. One needs some method of disrupting the sequence to allow another one to form. Lateral thinking is not an alternative to vertical thinking but an essential complement, which is made necessary by the nature of the information-processing system. Lateral thinking increases the effectiveness of vertical thinking by providing direction. One cannot look in the right direction by looking more efficiently in the wrong direction.

There are, however, situations in which the mere disruptive effect of lateral thinking is sufficient. Once certain myths and patterns have been disrupted then the formation of better patterns may follow on its own. Lateral thinking has nothing to do with chaos for the sake of chaos. Disruption of a pattern in lateral thinking is only in order to let a better pattern form. Later the process can be repeated again. For this reason those chemical methods of disruption which work by upsetting the smooth co-ordination of the mind are useless, since the smooth working of the mind is required to snap the new pattern into coherence. The art of lateral thinking is to bring about the disruption while still retaining the ability to benefit from it in terms of coherent ideas.

Lateral thinking is a deliberate form of thinking like the other forms. And like them it requires training and practice before it can be developed into an effective skill. A general awareness of the nature and need for lateral thinking is of some use, but it will more often help one to recognize when lateral thinking has brought something about than to use it deliberately. PO is a new word designed to allow lateral thinking to be used as habitually as logical thinking is used through the agency of NO. PO expresses the lateral thinking function which cannot properly be expressed in ordinary language without it.

The precise function of PO has been dealt with in Chapter 34. It allows such things as the juxtaposition of two ideas which have no logical, sequential or other connection at all. The purpose of the juxtaposition is not to make sense in itself, but to trigger off something else that will eventually make sense. PO has a nonsense function, but a deliberate nonsense function which is mathematically essential for the system. PO also counteracts the rigid and polarizing tendencies of the system.

In a way PO could be considered the zero of the language system. It has no value in itself, but it functions to make possible operations that would be impossible without it.

For real effectiveness, PO would have to be built into the training and education system, just as the right/wrong concept is at the moment.

It may be felt that far too much attention has been paid to mechanical information processes, and that too little attention has been paid to the 'feeling' processes which can easily override the information processes. As suggested before, it is the information processes that provide the aim for the gun that is fired by a powerful emotional charge. It is the information processes that give rise to the divisive tendencies, to the creating of differences where none exist, to the creating of myths and bogeys. It is the information processes that create the patterns and recognize them. It is quite true that once the emotional aspect has taken charge, then no amount of further information may be able to change the aim. But this is no more than the persistence of established patterns which in this case are especially well established by the emotional emphasis. It is the original pattern which allowed the channelling of emotion that matters, and this was at some time an information process.

Far from reducing the importance of emotions, the nature of the special memory-surface elevates them into an essential position. The special memory-surface is a passive system, and on it information organizes itself into patterns. The emotions (called internal patterns in previous sections) are the only contribution which the memory-surface makes to these information patterns. Thus emotion in its broadest sense provides the sole mechanism of adaptation whereby more useful patterns achieve dominance over neutral ones. Emotions also provide the substance of self and individuality. Without the emotional aspect, exactly identical information patterns would be formed on memory-surfaces which had had a similar exposure to information. On account of emotional variability these patterns may be very different.

These considerations are fairly obvious. What is less obvious is that even abstract intellectual processes such as logical thinking would be impossible without emotion. The whole NO reaction, without which logic would not work, is emotional at least in its origin, even if it eventually functions in a symbolic form. Early training in the emotional content of NO can conceivably make a big difference to the sort of thinking that is used later. Even apart from training, constitutional emotional variation may make a difference to the type of thinking that is available on different memory-surfaces. PO itself has an emotional content. All this is quite apart from the biasing and distorting effect which emotion can also exert on information-processing.

If information is the door that gives access to the world, then emotion is not just the paint on the door but the handle with which the door is opened. Emotion is essential to information-processing, not something apart. The division between intellect and emotion is another of the harmful polarizations that arise from the divisive tendencies of the system. Too often, emotion is thought of in terms of the caricatures and grotesqueries that are so often put forward as the stuff of emotion with the admirable purpose of attracting attention.

The artificial dichotomy between intellect and feeling creates a matched arrogance on either side. The feelers distrust the word-games of the intellectuals and the intellectuals distrust the aesthetic sighs of the feelers. The nature of the thinking process on the special memory-surface indicates that sequential thinking may be no more valid than non-sequential thinking. Therefore a feeling which is followed by a rationalization may be just as useful as a sequential approach. For example, the only useful ideas about freedom and justice arise as feelings first, which are then supported by reason and legislation. An intellectual approach ends up as a circular word-game. On the other hand the glorification of feeling as the only truth has led to the most damaging of passions.

The division between art and science is another of these polarizations. The two are but aspects of the same thing. Art is science with instant information. Science is art with progressive information. In both cases the aesthetics and the emotions are the same.

Since emotion is the major source of variability on the special memory-surface one might expect there to be an optimum level of emotionality for true creativity. At less than this level there would be too little change, at more than this level there would be too much fixity. It is true that the patterns fixed by over-emotionality might be worthwhile for their unusualness, but there would not be a creative fluidity about them.

The essential feature of the special memory-surface is that it is a passive system which provides an opportunity for information to organize itself. Much of the information comes from the environment, but a good deal is supplied by internal patterns which represent the needs and the emotions of the body that is using the memory-surface. The memory-surface comes to represent a biased record of cumulative experience of the environment. It is biased because it represents the interaction of the body and the environment. The limited area of activation moves over the memory-surface according to the contours of that surface. These contours are made up from an interaction of the internal patterns of the moment, what is being presented to the surface at the moment, and the record of what has happened in the past. Attention follows the movement of the area of activation. If one chooses to regard all the factors affecting the movement of attention as a 'self' which directs the attention, that is just another way of saying that attention passively follows the contours of the surface. The important point is that there is no separate agent which picks information out of the environment, stores it on the memory-surface then picks it off the surface in order to play around with it or use it.

The major theme of Eastern philosophy is the arbitrariness and artificiality of the separate units that have been carved out of the environment by the selfishness of the human spirit. The ultimate aim is to dissolve these separate units – and the self as one of them – back into the continuum of nature. Western philosophy, on the other hand, emphasizes the usefulness and sometimes the permanence of certain patterns. The ultimate aim is not to get rid of patterns, as in the East, but to achieve the right patterns.

A consideration of the information-handling processes on the special memory-surface makes one aware that the patterns on that surface are useful, but also fairly arbitrary. It is not a matter of decrying the deficiencies of the surface and getting rid of the patterns. Nor is it a matter of establishing the patterns as ends in themselves and enjoying their usefulness in that way. It is a matter of acknowledging the useful existence of the patterns but also being aware of the possibility of changing them to better patterns. So long as one is aware of this possibility then the dangers of arrogant fixity are lessened. As a symbol of the possibility of re-structuring the information contained in the current patterns, the word PO is convenient. As applied to the ideas of others it indicates the possible arrogance of their point of view. As applied to oneself it indicates the possible arrogance of an individual point of view.

And in that sense it can be applied to the ideas put forward in this book.

INDEX